GRANTA

VARGAS LLOSA FOR PRESIDENT

36

Editor: Bill Buford
Deputy Editor: Tim Adams
Managing Editor: Ursula Doyle
Editorial Assistant: Robert McSweeney
Contributing Editor: Lucretia Stewart

Managing Director: Derek Johns
Financial Controller: Geoffrey Gordon
Publishing Assistant: Sally Lewis

Picture Editor: Alice Rose George
Design: Chris Hyde
Executive Editor: Pete de Bolla
US Associate Publisher: Anne Kinard, Granta, 250 West 57th Street, Suite 1316, New York, NY 10107.

Editorial and Subscription Correspondence: Granta, 2–3 Hanover Yard, Noel Road, Islington, London N1 8BE. Telephone: (071) 704 9776. Fax: (071) 704 0474. Subscriptions: (071) 837 7765.
A one-year subscription (four issues) is £19.95 in Britain, £25.95 for the rest of Europe, and £31.95 for the rest of the world.
All manuscripts are welcome but must be accompanied by a stamped, self-addressed envelope or they cannot be returned.

Granta is published by Granta Publications Ltd and distributed by Penguin Books Ltd, Harmondsworth, Middlesex, England, Viking Penguin, a division of Penguin Books USA Inc, 375 Hudson Street, New York, NY 10014, USA; Penguin Books Australia Ltd, Ringwood, Victoria, Australia; Penguin Books Canada Ltd, 2801 John Street, Markham, Ontario, Canada L3R 1BR; Penguin Books (NZ) Ltd, 182–190 Wairau Road, Auckland 10, New Zealand.

The paper used in this publication meets the minimum requirements of American National Standard for Information Sciences—Permanence of Paper for Printed Library Materials, ANSI Z39.48-1984. ∞

Cover by Senate. Photo: Nubar Alexanian (Katz Pictures).

Granta 36, Summer 1991

ISBN 0-14-015206-7

Win a free trip to Thailand with the first annual Odyssey Guides WANDERING AUTHOR QUIZ

Everyone knows about great travel writers, but what about great writers who travel? The results can be very surprising, as readers of our new series of guidebooks will attest. Of the anecdotes that follow, some are found in our pages, others are imaginary, while others* almost *happened (but didn't). 'True' incidents have all been published in book form, although not necessarily written by their protagonists. To enter, please mail your answers to Odyssey Guides Draw, Hodder & Stoughton, Mill Road, Dunton Green, Sevenoaks, Kent TN13 2YA before September 1, 1991.

Only one entry per person is permitted. Entrants must be at least 18 years of age. Employees of Odyssey Guides, Hodder & Stoughton, associated companies, and their families are excluded. A draw will be conducted on September 20, 1991 and the first correct entry will receive **TWO ROUND-TRIP AIR TICKETS AND SEVEN NIGHTS' ACCOMMODATION IN THAILAND**. Fifty second prize winners will receive a set of four Odyssey Guides of their choice. Winners will be notified by October 10, 1991. A complete list of winners will be obtainable by writing to the address above.

ODYSSEY

Name ______________________________

Address ____________________________

____

T	F	
☐	☐	Jean-Paul Sartre rooting for the favourite at a kick-boxing match in Thailand
☐	☐	Aldous Huxley fleeing a stampede of sacred cows in Kashmir
☐	☐	Casanova witnessing an infant drown in the River Neva during a mass baptism in St Petersburg
☐	☐	Herman Hesse wandering until dawn through the red-light district of Singapore
☐	☐	Hans Christian Andersen extolling the humane virtues of Portuguese bullfighting
☐	☐	Ernest Hemingway oil wrestling the local champion under a carnival tent in Turkey
☐	☐	D H Lawrence sidestepping a rattlesnake at a Hopi snake dance in Arizona
☐	☐	Carlos Fuentes being harassed by a 200-pound grandmother in the Moscow subway
☐	☐	Salman Rushdie discussing the suppression of *Doctor Zhivago* with a Soviet bureaucrat in Nicaragua
☐	☐	Teddy Roosevelt declining a second helping of 1,000-year-old eggs in the Philippines
☐	☐	Gustave Flaubert fantasizing about lemon-ice while stranded in the Egyptian desert
☐	☐	Golda Meir caught in the middle of a frozen squid riot in Lisbon
☐	☐	Charlie Chaplin admiring the female form at a flagellation ceremony in Bali

ff

MILAN KUNDERA

Immortality

20th May 1991
0 571 14455 1 £14.99

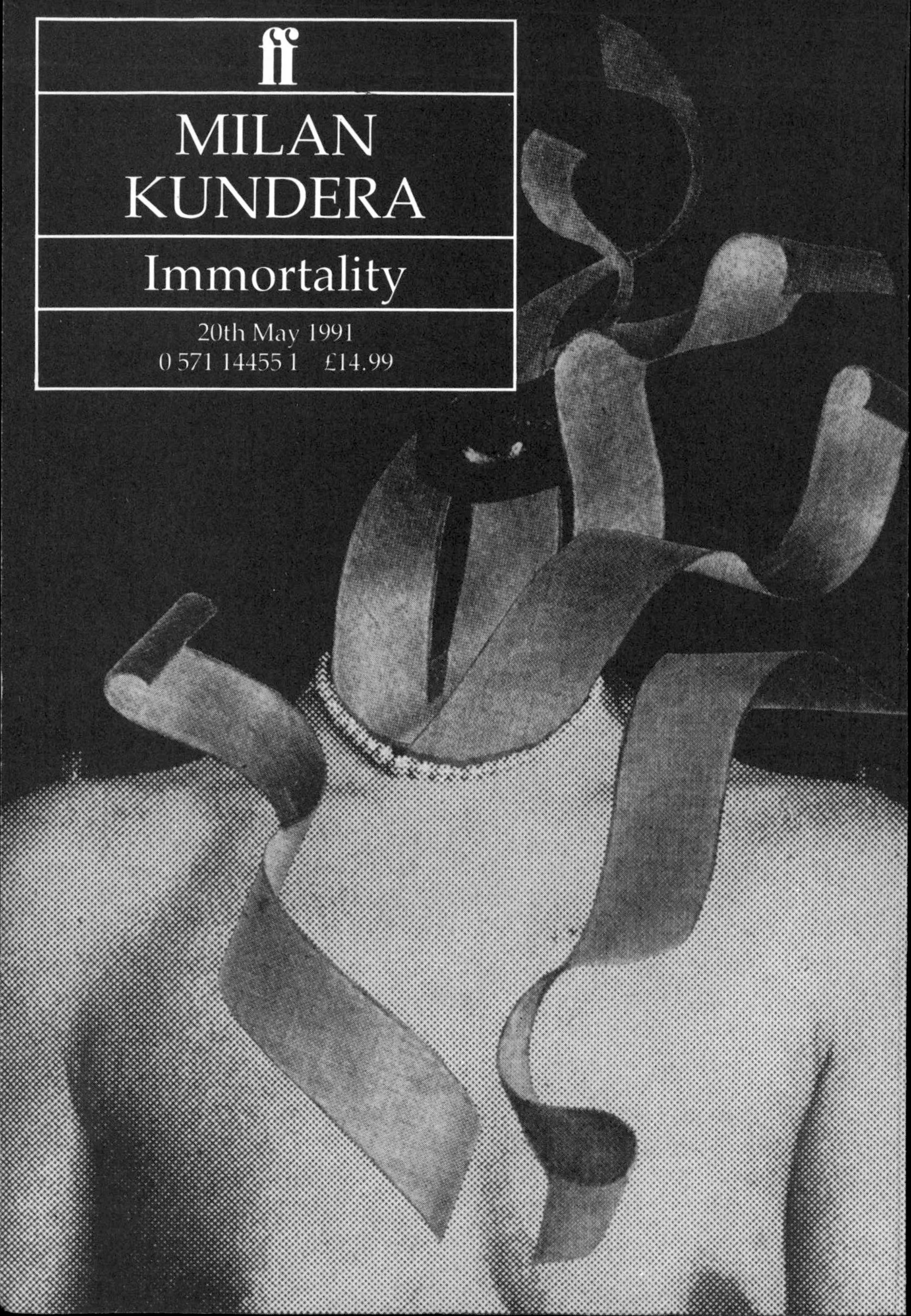

Contents

DEAD CERTAINTIES

(UNWARRANTED SPECULATIONS)

Simon Schama

GRANTA BOOKS

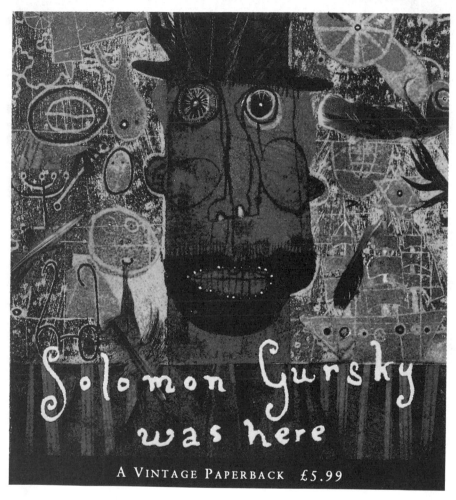

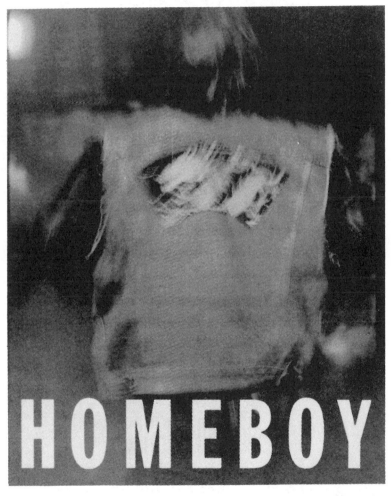

GRANTA

MARIO VARGAS LLOSA

A FISH OUT OF WATER

A Fish out of Water

At the end of July 1987, I was in the far north of Peru on a half-deserted beach where years before a young man from Piura and his wife had built several bungalows with the idea of renting them to tourists. Isolated, rustic, squeezed between stretches of sand, rock cliffs and the foamy waves of the Pacific, Punta Sal is one of the most beautiful sites in Peru. It is a place outside of time and history; its flocks of sea birds—gannets, pelicans, gulls, cormorants, ducks and albatrosses called *tijeretas* —parade in orderly formations from bright dawn to blood-red sunset. The fishermen of this remote corner of the Peruvian coast use simple rafts made in the same way as in pre-Hispanic times: two or three tree trunks tied together with a pole that serves as both oar and rudder. The sight of these rafts had greatly impressed me on my first visit to Punta Sal; they were identical in design and operation to the raft that, according to the *Chronicles of the Conquest*, Francisco Pizarro and his comrades found not far from here four centuries ago and considered to be the first proof that the imperial myth of gold that had drawn them from Panama to these shores was a reality.

I was in Punta Sal with Patricia and my children for National Holiday Week. We had returned to Peru not long before, from London, where we spend three months every year. I had intended to correct the proofs of my latest book, *El hablador*, between dips in the ocean, and to practice, from morning to night, the vice of solitude: reading.

I had turned fifty-one in March. All signs were that my life, unsettled from the day I was born, would become calm: a life spent between Lima and London, devoted exclusively to writing, with an occasional university stint in the United States. The previous year, I had dreamed up a 'five-year plan' of what I wanted to accomplish before my fifty-fifth birthday and had scribbled it in my memo-book.

One. A work for the theatre about a little, old Quixote-like man, who, in the Lima of the fifties, embarks on a crusade to save the city's colonial-era balconies that are threatened with demolition.

Two. A novel, something between a detective story and a fictional fantasy, about human sacrifices and political crimes in a village in the Andes.

Photo: Julio Etchart

Three. An essay on the gestation of Victor Hugo's *Les Misérables*.

Four. A play about an entrepreneur who, in a suite in the Savoy Hotel in London, meets his best friend from school, someone he thought had died but who has, thanks to hormones and surgery, turned into an attractive woman.

Five. An historical novel inspired by Flora Tristan, the Franco-Peruvian revolutionary, ideologist and feminist, who lived at the beginning of the nineteenth century.

In the same memo-book I had also jotted down less urgent projects: to learn that devilishly difficult language German; to live for a time in Berlin; to try, again, to get through books that had defeated me—*Finnegans Wake* and *The Death of Virgil*; to go down the Amazon from Pucallpa to Belem do Pará in Brazil; to bring out a revised edition of all my novels. Vague resolutions of a less publishable nature also figured on the list.

On the 28 July, at noon, I prepared to listen on a friend's little portable radio to the annual speech given by the President of the Republic to the Congress on the national holiday. Alan García had been in office for two years and was still very popular. For some his politics—a crude, populist socialism—were like a ticking bomb, waiting to explode. Populist policies had led to catastrophic failures in Salvador Allende's Chile and Siles Suazo's Bolivia; why should they succeed in Peru? García's policy had been to subsidize consumer spending by raising salaries and freezing prices, and it had brought a momentary prosperity: it would last only as long as the country had reserves of foreign currency available to allow for the purchase of imports that were essential for survival (Peru imports a large share of its food and its industrial components).

García's policies, however, were causing problems. Reserves were now on the point of being depleted, and García was unable to appeal to international financial institutions, having already alienated most of them by his confrontations with the International Monetary Fund and the World Bank. Moreover, his government had taken to printing paper money merely to cover its own debts. Inflation was worsening, and the dollar was being maintained at an artificially low rate (there were in fact any number of rates of exchange for the dollar, depending on the 'social necessity' of the product), discouraging exports and encouraging speculation and trading in contraband. García's policies were enriching only a handful of people, while sinking the rest of the country's population into poverty that was increasing by the day.

I had only one interview with Alan García while he was president. I had arrived from London and had been met by one of his aides-de-camp whom García had sent to welcome me back. It was the protocol that I then went to the government palace to thank the president for the courtesy. Alan García received me personally, and our meeting lasted for an hour and a half. He showed me a handmade bazooka, put together by *Sendero Luminoso*—Shining Path, the Maoist guerrilla movement —which had been used to launch a projectile against the palace. He was young and, as a good politician should, knew how to turn on the charm. I had met him only once before, during his election campaign, over dinner at the home of a mutual friend. The impression I left with was of a man driven by his attraction to power and who would do anything to get it. I then appeared on television and said that I wouldn't be voting for him, but for Luis Bedoya Reyes, the candidate of the Christian Popular Party. And, later still, I would write an open letter to him once he was in power, condemning him for the massacre of rioters in the Lima prisons in June 1986 (hundreds of inmates in three prisons, all members of *Sendero Luminoso*, rose up in protest and revolt and were summarily killed—even after some had surrendered to the prison authorities). But, despite all this, despite my evident opposition to his policies, García did not bear me any ill will (in fact, at the beginning of his term, he had asked me to accept the ambassadorship to Spain). I said to him, jokingly, that it was a shame that he was determined to be Peru's Salvador Allende, or Fidel Castro, when he had the chance to be its Felipe González.

In our meeting, García went into great detail describing his objectives for the forthcoming year, illustrating them on a blackboard. One objective he did not mention was the most important. That was the one I would learn about later, listening to García's annual speech to the Congress on that hot day on the beach of Punta Sal, his voice crackling and broken on the ancient radio: his initiative to nationalize and bring under government control all banks, insurance companies and financial institutions.

I heard this announcement while standing beside an elderly man. He was wearing a bathing-suit and a leather glove that hid an artificial hand. 'Eighteen years ago,' he said, 'I read in the papers that General Velasco had taken my country estate away from me. Now, on this little radio, I hear that Alan García has taken my company away from me.'

He rose to his feet and dived into the ocean. Most of the vacationers in Punta Sal that day did not take the news in the same debonair spirit. They were professionals, executives and a few businessmen who were actually associated with the threatened companies. But like the man with the artificial hand, they remembered the dictatorship, twelve years (1968–80) of massive nationalizations. At the beginning of the military regime there were seven nationalized industries; at the end there were over 200. In the name of a socialist participatory democracy, General Juan Velasco Alvarado had nationalized the petroleum, electricity, mining and sugar industries. Peru, when Velasco came to power, was a poor country; he turned it into a poverty-stricken one. Now, as in a recurrent nightmare, Alan García's 'democratic socialism' was about to gobble up banks, insurance companies and financial firms.

At a gloomy meal that evening, the woman at the next table lamented her fate: her husband, one of many Peruvians who had emigrated, had given up a good position in Venezuela to return to Lima—to take over the management of a bank! Would they have to leave Peru again?

'Once more Peru has taken a step backwards, towards barbarism,' I remember telling Patricia the next morning. We were going for a run along the beach, escorted by a rectilinear flock of gannets. The nationalizations would increase the

Opposite: Alan García, on winning the presidential elections in 1985.

Photo: Julio Etchart

85 TE SALUDA
PRESIDENTE
PRESENTE

poverty, parasitism and bribery of Peruvian life. Sooner or later they will fatally damage the democratic government that Peru was able to retrieve in 1980, after twelve years of military rule.

'Why the fuss,' I have often been asked, 'over a few nationalizations? Mitterand nationalized the banks in France: even though the measure was a failure French democracy was never endangered.' It is a reasonable point, but it is also one that betrays an ignorance of underdevelopment, which is characterized by its blurring of the roles of the government and the state. In France, Sweden or Britain the public sector has a degree of autonomy in its dealings with those who hold political power; it belongs to the state and its administration, and its personnel and their functions are more or less safe from misuse by the government of the day. In an underdeveloped country, as in a totalitarian one, the government *is* the state, and those in power administrate it as though it were their own private property, their spoils: the institutions of the public sector provide cushy jobs for protégés and serve to feed people under their patronage. Such institutions turn into bureaucratic swarms paralyzed by the corruption and inefficiency imposed upon them by politics. They never go broke, being monopolies subsidized against competition by the taxpayer's money (the deficit of running the public sector in Peru in 1988 was 2.5 billion dollars, which equalled foreign currency brought in by exports for the year).

Nobody likes bankers. They symbolize affluence, selfish capitalism, imperialism, all causes of Third World wretchedness and backwardness. Alan García had found, in financiers, the ideal scapegoat for the failure of his programmes: the financial oligarchies had removed their dollars from Peru and made secret loans out of the savings accounts of others to their own companies. With the financial system in the hands of the people, everything would change.

'The worst of it is,' I said to Patricia, panting, as we finished our four-kilometre run, 'this proposal will be supported by ninety-nine per cent of Peruvians.'

I returned to Lima from Punta Sal and wrote an article, 'Towards a Totalitarian Peru', that appeared in *El Comercio* on 2 August. I wanted to put on record my opposition to nationalizing the country's financial institutions, and the article, outlining my reasons, urged Peruvians to oppose the nationalizations as well, using every legal means possible, if they wanted to see our democracy preserved. I doubted that my article would have much effect; I assumed the nationalization measure would be passed by Congress and supported by the majority of Peruvians.

But I was wrong.

My article appeared on the very day that the employees in the banks and the other threatened services actually took to the streets in Lima, in Arequipa, in Piura. I was astonished, as was everyone else. With four close friends—the architects Luis Miró Quesada, Freddy Cooper and Miguel Cruchaga, and the painter Fernando de Szyszlo—we went a step further and drafted a manifesto and collected a hundred signatures. I read the text on television; it appeared, with my name at the head, in the daily papers the next day, on 3 August, under the banner 'Opposing the Totalitarian Threat'. The manifesto stated that 'the concentration of political and economic power in the party in power might well mean the end of freedom of expression and, eventually, of democracy.'

In the next few days my life was changed. There were letters and phone calls and an endless number of supporters of the manifesto visiting my house, bringing piles of signatures they had collected. The names of hundreds of new supporters appeared every day in the media not controlled by the government. People from the provinces stunned me with offers of help. After twenty years of nationalized industry now, in these feverish days of August 1987, significant sectors of Peruvian society seemed to have rejected the formula of government control.

The next week my friends Freddy Cooper and Felipe Thorndike visited me at home. Felipe Thorndike, an entrepreneur and petroleum engineer, had been a victim of General Velasco's dictatorship, which had expropriated all his holdings, and he had been obliged to go into exile. While abroad, he rebuilt his businesses and, in 1980, returned to Peru determined to work in his native country. Felipe Thorndike and Freddy Cooper had been having meetings with political independents—the majority of Peruvians refuse to be affiliated with any one of the innumerable political parties—and they proposed that we call for a public demonstration at the Plaza San Martín, the big square in Lima. They wanted to call the demonstration a 'Meeting for Freedom', and asked me if I would be the main speaker. The idea was to show that not only could members of the left take to the streets to defend state control, but we could also, to defend freedom. I accepted.

That night I had the first of a series of arguments with Patricia that were to go on for a year.

'If you go on to that platform you'll end up going into politics, and literature will go to hell, and your family along with it. Don't you know what it means to go into politics in this country?'

'I headed the protest against nationalization. I can't back down now. It's only one demonstration, one speech. It doesn't mean I'll devote my life to politics.'

'There'll be more demonstrations and you'll end up being a candidate. Are you going to leave your books, the quiet life you're living now, to go into politics in Peru? Don't you know how they're going to pay you back?'

'I'm not going to go into politics or give up literature or be a candidate for office. I'm going to speak at one demonstration, to show that not all Peruvians have been taken in by Alan García.'

'They'll burn down our house, they'll bomb us, they'll kidnap the children and kill you. Don't you know what kind of thugs you're picking as enemies? I've noticed that you've stopped answering the phone.'

It was true. The anonymous calls had started the day the manifesto was published. They came during the day and at night. To get to sleep we had to disconnect the phone. The voices were different each time. I came to think that it was every García supporter's idea of fun, once he'd had a drink, to call my house to announce that at any time he and his friends were going to cut off my balls, rape Patricia and my daughter Morgana and cut up my sons' faces with knives. The calls continued for nearly three years. They became part of the family routine. When, at the time of the elections, they stopped, a sort of vacuum, a nostalgia even, lingered on in the house.

The Plaza San Martín demonstration was set for the next week, 21 August. The days leading up to the demonstration were intense and exhausting, and in retrospect, the most exciting I experienced. So many people had volunteered to help—collecting money, printing pamphlets and placards, preparing pennants, lending their homes for meetings, offering transportation for the demonstrators and driving through the streets in vehicles with loud-speakers. My home was a madhouse, and on the evening of 21 August I hid out for a few hours at the home of Carlos and Maggie, two friends, to prepare the first political speech of my life (Carlos was later kidnapped, by members of the Túpac Amaru Revolutionary Movement and held in captivity for six months in a tiny cellar without ventilation). I made a point of asking shareholders of the threatened companies and members of the two principal opposition parties—Popular Action and the Christian Popular Party—not to become involved so that the demonstration could clearly be seen as an event of principle, a protest by Peruvians who had taken to the streets to defend not personal or political interests but the very values that would be endangered by nationalization.

In the event, not even the most optimistic among us could have predicted what happened that night. The numbers were extraordinary. There were people packed so tightly into the Plaza San Martín, elbow to elbow, that they overflowed into the neighbouring streets. And when I then stepped up to the platform I felt something strange. It was a mix of joy and terror. The spectacle before me was awesome to contemplate. Tens of thousands of people—a hundred thousand at least—were waving flags and singing at the top of their lungs the 'Hymn to Freedom', which had been written for the occasion by Augusto

---

Overleaf: Mario Vargas Llosa at the end of his speech at the Plaza San Martín, 21 August 1987.

Polo Campos, a popular composer. I said that economic freedom was inseparable from political freedom, and this vast crowd fervently applauded. I said that private property and a market economy were the only guarantees of development, and the applause increased. I said that we Peruvians would not allow our democratic system 'to be Mexicanized' or let Alan García's Apra Party become the Trojan Horse of communism. The response was deafening, enveloping, unanimous. Something had changed in Peru.

I had been assigned bodyguards, and there was an incident as I was leaving the Plaza. A private protection agency known as 'The Israelis'—its owners came from Israel—was in charge of protecting us. Manuel and Alberto, two ex-Marines, had accompanied me to the Plaza and stood at the foot of the speaker's platform. When I finished, I invited the crowd to go with me to the Palace of Justice to hand over to the members of Congress the signatures against nationalization. During the march, Manuel disappeared, swallowed up by the crowd. But Alberto stuck to me like glue. We were nearly crushed by the demonstrators. Suddenly a black car drove up with its doors open. I was lifted off my feet and put inside. Armed men surrounded me. I assumed that they were 'The Israelis'. But then I heard Alberto yelling: 'It's not them, it's not them!' and saw him struggle. He dived into the car just as it was driving off and landed like a dead weight on top of me and the other occupants.

'Is this a kidnapping?' I asked, half jokingly, half seriously.

'Our job is to look after you,' the bruiser-driver answered. Then he spoke into his hand radio: 'The Jaguar is safe and we're going to the moon. Over.'

It was Oscar Balbi of Prosegur, a competitor of 'The Israelis'. Its president, Juan Jochamowitch, had decided, without anyone's asking, to protect me and my house.

I had become a politician.

It is said that when Alan García saw the rally on his television that night he smashed the screen in a fit of rage. Because of the rally at the Plaza San Martín the nationalization law, although already passed in Congress, where García's supporters had an absolute majority, would never be put into effect. It was a death blow to Alan García's political ambition—he had hopes of remaining in the office of president for an unlimited time—and it opened the doors of Peruvian political life to liberal thought that until then had lacked a way of expressing itself publicly (our modern history has always been dominated by extremes—the ideological populism of conservatives or socialists of various tendencies). It gave the initiative back to the opposition parties, which following their defeat in 1985 had passed into a kind of oblivion.

In the meanwhile, Patricia's fears were confirmed. Five days later we held another rally in Arequipa, on 26 August. Again thousands attended, but there was also violence. We were assaulted by counter-demonstrators from García's Apra Party—the famous 'buffaloes', the armed hoodlums of the party—and by members of a Maoist faction of the United Left, the *Patria Roja* (Red Fatherland). They set off explosives and, armed with clubs, stones and stink-bombs, launched an attack just as I was beginning to speak in the hope of starting a stampede. The young people in charge of maintaining order on the outer edge of the Plaza resisted, but several were wounded.

'Do you see? Do you see?' Patricia said that night. She had been obliged to dive underneath a policeman's riot shield to escape a shower of bottles. 'What I was afraid of has already started happening.' But despite her opposition in principle, she worked morning and night organizing our meetings.

2

At the end of September 1987, all the people involved in organizing the rally were summoned by Freddy Cooper to Fernando de Szyszlo's studio. There, amid half-finished paintings and masks and pre-Hispanic feather cloaks, we developed the ideas that would be the foundation of a new freedom movement: *Libertad*. We wanted to create something that was broader and more flexible than a political party, a movement that would unite everyone who had opposed nationalization, particularly the *informales*, the members of the 'informal' economy—the millions of peasants who, unable to participate in the state's economy, had created their own black market, popular capitalism. We wanted a comprehensive programme of political reform.

We spent hours under the bewitching spell of Szyszlo's paintings, discussing a plan for governing Peru, and the programme we settled on was one that would revolutionize Peru's economic and social structures and put an end to privileges, government hand-outs, protectionism, state control, and create a free society, in which everyone would have access to the market and be able to live under the protection of the law. The programme was characterized by our firm determination to change things, by our resolve to do away with poverty so that every Peruvian could attain a decent life. The programme fills me with pride even now. I contributed only 'moral support', the work being done by Lucho Bustamante, Raúl Salazar and dozens of others who devoted countless days and nights to preparing the first rough outline of a new country. It was marvellous to witness. Each time I attended these planning meetings, even the most technical ones—on reforming the mining industry or the practices of the customs office or the port authority or the judicial systems—I felt vindicated: politics had become a task requiring intellect, imagination, idealism, generosity.

In preparing our programme, we attracted engineers, architects, attorneys, physicians, entrepreneurs, economists—people who had not entered politics before and had no wish to be political activists in the future. They were professionals, who loved their profession and wanted to be able to practice it freely. They entered politics reluctantly at the beginning and became active when persuaded that it was only with their co-operation that we could make Peruvian politics into something that was decent and efficient.

Between the first meeting in Szyszlo's studio and the opening of the *Libertad* headquarters on 15 March 1988, we worked long and hard, but without a plan, feeling our way. None of us had any experience, and I had less than my friends. I had spent my life in a study, inventing tales in fanatical solitude; it was not the best preparation for organizing a political movement. Miguel

Cruchaga, *Libertad*'s first Secretary General, had likewise lived shut up in his architect's studio and was most unsociable. He was in no position to make up for my ineffectiveness. He was, however, the first to give up his profession and devote himself full time to the Movement. Others would do the same, managing a living on the small amounts that *Libertad* could pay them.

My greatest ambition was to attract young people and show them that the real revolution for a country like ours would be one that replaced arbitrariness with the rule of law, and convince them that liberal reform could make Peru a prosperous modern country. It was also one of our goals to retrieve the intellectuals, journalists and politicians who, arguing against socialists and populists and the practices of paternalism and protectionism, had once defended liberalism. To this end we organized our *Libertad* days—the *Jornadas de la Libertad.*

These were talks—they lasted from nine in the morning till nine at night—that allowed us to illustrate how nationalization had impoverished the country and how government control had not only destroyed our industries but went against all of our interests, favouring small mafias with a system of quotas and preferential dollar exchange rates. There were talks devoted to explaining the 'parallel economy' of the *informales* and defending its itinerant pedlars, artisans and tradesmen, small-scale business people of modest origins, who in many fields had proved themselves to be more efficient than the state and, sometimes, even large-scale entrepreneurs. A recurrent theme was the necessity of reforming the state and strengthening it by paring away its excesses. There was talk, too, about the four 'Asian dragons'—South Korea, Taiwan, Hong Kong and Singapore (or, separately, Chile)—Third World countries which had market-oriented policies, promoting exports and private enterprise, but whose repressive governments were in flagrant contradiction of every other kind of liberal reform. This was neither acceptable nor necessary. Freedom had to be understood as a principle that was indivisible, politically and economically, and that was, therefore, the *raison d'être* of the Movement itself: we wanted an electoral mandate from the Peruvian people that would allow us to enshrine this principle in a democratic civilian regime. The point I defended most forcefully was always this—*a great liberal reform is possible under democratic rule, provided that a clear majority votes for it, and to achieve it, it is essential to be open and honest, explaining in detail what we want to do and the price we would exact for it. Only in this way would we have the power necessary for 'the great change'.*

We tried to draw a distinction between 'movement' and 'party', but it was a distinction that turned out to be too subtle for Peruvian political habits. For, despite its name, the *Movimiento Libertad* was from the start indistinguishable from a party. The majority of our followers assumed it was one, and it was impossible to disabuse them of this notion. Laughable situations arose, symptomatic of a national psychology deeply rooted in the tradition of *clientelismo.* Every party used the *carnet*—the individual membership book carried by its members—as a way of giving party members preference when it came to government jobs and favours. We decided that the Movement would not have any *carnets.* Writing one's name on a list on a plain sheet of paper was all that would be required to sign up as a member.

It was impossible to get this idea across, particularly in the areas where our followers felt that their status was inferior to that of Alan García's followers, the Apristas, or the communists or the socialists, who were able to show off impressive-looking *carnets* full of seals and stamps in bright colours. Our own Executive Committee began to pressure us to issue *carnets.* Again and again we argued that we wanted to be different from other parties and that we wanted to prevent a *Libertad carnet*, if we came to power, from being abused in the future. It was no use. I discovered that in certain city districts and towns our committees had begun to give out *carnets*, each of them loaded with little flags and signatures, and some of them even bearing my photograph! Our arguments of principle had been subordinated to the arguments of the activists: 'If they aren't given a *carnet*, they won't sign up.' So at the end of the campaign there was not just one *Libertad carnet*, but a whole heterogeneous collection of them, invented by various local headquarters to suit themselves.

3

Whenever I'm asked why I was ready to give up my vocation as a writer—what I love most in the world—for the trifling and often contemptible activity that politics had once seemed to me to be, I answer: 'For a moral reason.'

Circumstances placed me in a position of leadership at a critical moment in the life of my country. It appeared that, supported by a majority of Peruvians, there was an opportunity to accomplish the liberal reforms which I had defended in articles and polemical exchanges since the early 1970s.

Patricia doesn't see it that way. 'The moral obligation wasn't the decisive factor,' she says. 'It was the adventure, the illusion of an experience full of excitement and risk. Of writing the great novel in real life.'

This may be the truth. If the presidency of Peru had not been, as I said jokingly to a journalist, 'the most dangerous job in the world,' I might not have become a candidate. If the decadence, impoverishment, terrorism and constant crises had not made governing the country an almost impossible challenge, it would never have entered my head to take on the task.

But if adventure played its part, so, too, did something else. I don't want to be grandiloquent, but I shall call it the moral commitment.

Let me try to explain something that is not easy to explain without lapsing into clichés or political rhetoric. I detest nationalism; I see it as a human aberration that has caused much blood to flow; I agree with Dr Johnson that patriotism is 'the last refuge of a scoundrel.' I have lived a good part of my life abroad and have never felt like a total stranger anywhere. But the relations I have with the country of my birth are more intimate and long-lasting than those I have with any other, including the countries in which I have come to feel completely at home: England, France and Spain. Events in Peru affect me more—make me happier or more angry—than events elsewhere. I cannot justify rationally what I feel: that between me and Peruvians of all races, languages and social strata there is an inviolable bond. Does this stem from my childhood in Bolivia, in an expatriate household, where my mother and grandparents and aunts and uncles considered Peru, the fact of being Peruvian, as the most precious gift ever bestowed on a family?

It is less exact to say that I love my country than that it is continually in my thoughts and a constant mortification. I cannot free myself from it, and it grieves me deeply. It grieves me to see that, for many years now, it has interested the rest of the world only because of the cataclysms that trouble its geography, the record rates of its inflation, the activities of its drug-traders or its terrorist massacres. It is spoken of outside its borders—when spoken of at all—as a horrible caricature of a country that is slowly dying because of the inability of Peruvians to govern themselves with even the minimum of common sense. George Orwell, in his beautiful essay 'The Lion and the Unicorn', says that England is a family with 'the wrong members in control.' How well that definition applies to Peru! Is it not true that among us are decent people capable of doing, for example, what the Spaniards have done with Spain in the last ten years? But such people have seldom gone into politics, a realm that almost always has been in dishonest and mediocre hands in Peru.

At several periods in my life, before the events of August 1987, I had lost hope in Peru. But hope for what? When I was younger, it was the hope that, in one leap, Peru would become a prosperous, modern and cultivated country. Later, it was then the hope that, before I died, Peru would have begun to eradicate poverty, backwardness, injustice and violence, and that progress, no matter how rapid or how slow, would give every appearance of being irreversible.

Countries today can choose to be prosperous. The most harmful myth of our time, now deeply embedded in the consciousness of the Third World, is that poor countries live in poverty because of a conspiracy of the rich countries which have arranged things to keep them underdeveloped, in order to exploit them. In the past, prosperity depended almost exclusively on geography and power. But the internationalization of life—of markets, technology, capital—today permits any country, if organized on a competitive basis, to achieve rapid growth. In the last two decades, Latin America has *chosen* to go backwards, by practising, through its dictatorships or bureaucratic populism, a kind of economic nationalism. And Peru has gone even further back than any other Latin American country. The political parties might disagree how much state intervention was desirable, but all of them appeared to accept that state intervention of some kind was necessary and that without it neither progress nor social justice was possible. The modernization of Peru seemed to me to have been put off till pigs had wings.

The Peru of my childhood was always poor: in the last decades, it has become poorer still. A region I have always known well is the *departamento* of Piura. I lived there as a child and an adolescent, and have travelled in it a fair amount, first with my grandfather and later with my uncle Lucho, who had a smallholding in the Chira Valley where he grew cotton. I returned recently and couldn't believe my eyes. The little towns in the provinces of Sullana and Paita, or those in the mountains and the desert, seemed to have died a living death: they languish in hopeless apathy. It is true, in my memory, that the dwellings were always crude, made of clay and wild cane, that people went barefoot, that the roads were bad and that there were no medical dispensaries, schools, water or electricity. But in these poor small towns of my childhood, there had been at least a powerful vitality—a light-heartedness, energy, hope—that now had died out entirely.

Piura illustrates the nineteenth-century naturalist Antonio Raimondi's description of Peru as 'a beggar sitting on a bench made of gold.' It shows how a country *chooses* underdevelopment. Off the coast of Piura is a wealth of fish; offshore, there is oil; in the desert there are immense phosphate mines that are yet to be worked; the soil, having once produced cotton, rice and fruit on its landed estates, is one of the most fertile in Peru. Why should an area with these resources die of starvation?

General Velasco confiscated the large landed estates where, in fact, the workers received a very small percentage of the profits, and turned them into co-operatives, 'social properties', where the peasants were meant eventually to replace the former owners. They did not. The owners were replaced by directors who ended up exploiting the peasants as much, if not more than, their predecessors. In the past, however, the owners, knowing how to work the land, also knew to re-invest profits and replace worn-out machinery; the new heads of the co-operatives did not, with the result that there were no profits to share (in the sixties, Peru's income *per capita* from animal husbandry was the second highest in Latin America; in 1990, it was the second lowest; only Haiti's was worse).

Commercial fishing is another example. In the fifties, thanks to the vision and energy of a group of entrepreneurs, a great industry emerged on the Peruvian coast: the manufacture of fish meal. In a few years Peru became the number one producer in the world. Dozens of factories were built. Thousands of jobs were created, and the little port of Chimbote was transformed into a large commercial and industrial centre, developing commercial fishing to such an extent that by the 1970s Peru had a larger fishing industry than Japan.

Velasco's military dictatorship nationalized the fisheries and made them into a gigantic conglomerate—*Pesca Perú*—which he put in the hands of a bureaucracy. The industry was ruined. By 1987, fish meal factories had closed in La Libertad, Piura, Chimbote, Lima, Ica and Arequipa. And while boats of the conglomerate rotted in the harbours for lack of spare parts, the conglomerate itself received huge state subsidies, further impoverishing the nation. It has now been closed. When I heard that the inhabitants of Atico, a little town on the coast of Arequipa, had gathered, with their mayor at the head, to plead for the 'privatization' of the fish meal factory, I flew there to show the townspeople that my sympathies lay with them. I remembered that the harbour had been bustling with fishing smacks and small sea-going boats and that the streets had been jammed with *camareros*—refrigerator trucks—that crossed the vast desert for the anchovies and other fish needed by the factories in Chimbote. I was taken aback by what I found when I arrived; the coast was overcome by inertia.

Meanwhile the deposits of oil remain underground. The

wells were once run by the Belco Oil Company, but the company became involved in litigation with the government. And so, during his first year in office, Alan García simply nationalized the oil company: end of dispute. Having been an exporter of petroleum, Peru now needs to import it.

There are reasons why no one extends credits to Peru, why no one invests.

On 3 June 1990, I had a public debate with my adversary. Alberto Fujimori gibed: 'It seems that you would like to make Peru a Switzerland, Doctor Vargas Llosa?' I admitted that the idea did not displease me. Fujimori smiled; he had won a point. Wanting to see Peru made into 'a Switzerland' came to be, for a considerable number of my compatriots, a grotesque goal. But on that night of 21 August 1987, standing before the deliriously enthusiastic crowd in the Plaza San Martín, I had the impression—the certainty—that there were hundreds of thousands, perhaps millions, of Peruvians who had suddenly decided to do the impossible and make Peru 'a Switzerland' some day, a country without the poor or the unemployed or the illiterate, a country of cultured, prosperous and free people, and that they had decided to bring about this change without bullets, with nothing but votes and laws, within the framework of democracy.

4

All over Peru people began to talk of the alliance: the democratic forces opposed to both Apra, García's once revolutionary party, and the United Left, the coalition of communists and socialists, who had won the 1985 elections. In Lima members of the two opposition parties, Popular Action and the Christian Popular Party, were starting to join our movement of independents. The same thing happened in Piura and Arequipa.

I visited, separately, the leaders of both parties: Fernando Belaúnde Terry of Popular Action, who had himself twice been elected president, once having been deposed by a military dictatorship and once being the successor to it (when, despite popular support, he did little to remedy the disasters of the previous regime); and Luis Bedoya Reyes of the Christian Popular Party, the candidate I had supported against García in the elections of 1985. Both Belaúnde and Bedoya expressed support for the idea of working together, and after a series of lengthy and sometimes tense meetings, we agreed to set up a tripartite commission that would co-ordinate an alliance between us. Three delegates would represent Popular Action; three, the Christian Popular Party; and three other 'independents' would represent the *Libertad* movement of which I was the recognized leader.

Many have criticized me for forming an alliance with two traditional parties which had already been in power (for a good part of Belaúnde's two terms as president, Bedoya had been his ally). This alliance, my critics maintain, compromised the freshness of my candidacy and made it appear to be an instrument of the old bosses of the Peruvian right.

'How could Peruvians have believed in the "great change" that you offered,' I was asked, 'if you linked arms with those who governed the country between 1980 and 1985, without changing a thing that had been going badly? When you joined up with Belaúnde and Bedoya you committed suicide.'

I was aware of the risks, but I decided that they were outweighed by the benefits of an alliance. Many reforms were needed in Peru, and, to see them through, a broad popular base was required. Popular Action and the Christian Popular Party had impeccable democratic credentials and could influence significant sectors of the populace. To present ourselves to voters as separate parties would split support between the centre and right and make either United Left or Apra the winner. The negative image of 'old pols' could be effaced with our new programme, reforms that had nothing to do with the populism of Popular Action or the conservatism of the Christian Popular Party but that would be associated with a radical liberalism never before put forward in Peru. Perhaps, most important, *Libertad* consisted mainly of members with no political experience—there was no party apparatus—and we needed help from the established parties merely to compete with both Apra (which in addition to its own organization could also depend on the machinery of the state in its campaign) and a left that had been battle-hardened in a number of elections.

5

Over a three-year period I met with Belaúnde and Bedoya several times a month. At the beginning we met in different places to avoid reporters; later we met principally at my house, in the morning, around ten o'clock. Bedoya would arrive late, which irritated Belaúnde, who was always punctual and eager for the meetings to end so he could go off to the Club Regatas to swim and play badminton (he sometimes came with his training-shoes and racket).

It is hard to imagine that there could be two politicians so different from each other. Bedoya came from humble origins—his family was lower middle class—and he had worked long and hard to be able to carve out a career as an attorney. He was not, however, a good speaker and, worse, was given to making impetuous statements in public. His political career had had a brief apogee—he was Lima's magnificent mayor during Belaúnde's first term—but afterwards he could do nothing to shake off the labels of 'reactionary', 'defender of the oligarchy' or 'man of the extreme right' that the left pinned on him. He ran for president in 1980 (against Belaúnde among others) and again in 1985 (against García) and was defeated both times. Peruvians were never going to allow him to head their government.

Bedoya's long-winded, courtroom-style soliloquies used to infuriate Belaúnde, uninterested as he was in ideologies and doctrines and constitutionally allergic to anything abstract (the ideology of his Popular Action party consisted of an elementary imitation of Roosevelt's New Deal—a great many public works projects—nationalistic slogans such as 'The conquest of Peru by Peruvians' and romantic allusions to the empire of the Incas and the pre-Hispanic people of the Andes). But of the two, Bedoya proved to be the more flexible: he was the one ready to make concessions for the sake of the alliance that we were trying to forge between the three of us, and once we had arrived at an agreement, he could be counted on to fulfil it to the letter. Belaúnde always conveyed the sense that the alliance was there to serve his Popular Action, and Bedoya and I were merely two bit players. Beneath his elegant manners, there was vanity and stubbornness and a touch of the *caudillo* accustomed to doing and undoing whatever he pleased without anybody in his party daring to contradict him. Belaúnde, born to an aristocratic family (although not a wealthy one), had reached the winter of his life heaped with honours: he had been president twice and was seen to be an upright, democratic statesman, an image that not even his most bitter adversary could deny him. He was a good public speaker with a splendid nineteenth-century rhetorical style, a man of melodramatic gestures—fighting a duel, for instance. When he had suddenly emerged as a public figure in the last years of General Odría's dictatorship (1948–56), he was seen as a reformer, determined to make social changes and modernize Peru. When he became president in 1963, he stirred up enormous hope. But his administration accomplished little and the military *coup* by General Velasco in 1968 sent Belaúnde into exile in the United States, where he lived during the dictatorship, very modestly, teaching. Perhaps his one strength was being able to survive until the next election because in every other respect—and above all in economic policy—he was a failure. During his second term as president (1980–85), the national debt increased dangerously, corruption contaminated his administration and inflation raged unchecked. Belaúnde also failed to confront terrorism: at the time it was only beginning and could have been stopped.

I voted for Belaúnde every time he ran, although I was aware of his shortcomings. I defended him during his second term. After twelve years of dictatorship the reconstruction of democracy was the first priority, and I felt it could be best attained if Popular Action was returned to power. Belaúnde, a man of decency, has two qualities that are not often found in a Peruvian politician: a genuine belief in democracy and absolute honesty (when he left the government palace he was poorer than when he entered it); but I refused, with one exception, all the posts he offered me: embassies in London and in Washington, the ministries of education and foreign relations and, finally, the office of prime minister. The exception was my unpaid, month-long appointment to the commission investigating the killing of eight journalists in Uchuraccay, a remote region of the Andes, an appointment for which I was mercilessly attacked and slandered for months by the press and which gave Patricia and me nightmares.*

It was during Belaúnde's second term that he summoned me unexpectedly to the government palace one night. He is a reserved man who never reveals his intimate thoughts. But on this occasion—over the next few months we would have another two or three meetings—he spoke explicitly and with emotion, allowing me to glimpse the subjects that were tormenting him. He had appointed financial experts to manage the country's economy, had given them license to do whatever they wanted, and he was deeply distressed by the result. History would not remember the advisors; it would remember him. Moreover, some of their advisors were insisting on being paid in dollars at a time when everyone else was being asked to make sacrifices. There was melancholy and bitterness in his voice and in his silences.

What would happen to Peru after the 1985 election? he wanted to know. He could see that his own party wouldn't win, nor would the Christian Popular Party, since Bedoya lacked the power to draw people at the polls. This would mean the triumph of Apra, with Alan García as president. The consequences were frightful. 'Peru,' Belaúnde said that night, 'has no idea what that young man may be capable of if he comes to power.' He must be stopped and could be stopped, Belaúnde said, if I were the candidate of Popular Action and the Popular Christian Party. He thought I would attract the independent vote. He countered my protestations that I was no good at politics (as time would confirm) with flattery and kindness—I would even say affection, if this word were not so much at odds with Belaúnde's sober, unemotional personality.

*The account of the killing of eight journalists, 'The Story of a Massacre', is published in *Granta* 9.

Bedoya once described Belaunde as 'a master at taking the syringe out of his backside,' and in fact it was impossible to pin him down or discuss any subject that wasn't to his liking. He always managed to slip off at a tangent, telling anecdotes about his travel—he had an encyclopaedic knowledge of the country's geography, having been all over Peru on foot, on horseback, in a canoe—or about his two terms in office, without giving anyone the chance to interrupt him, and then would look suddenly at his watch, get to his feet—'Well, just look how late it's got'—bid us goodbye and disappear.

It is not surprising that in the three years I never once talked with Belaúnde and Bedoya about the Alliance's policy for running the country. We knew that the parties in the alliance had different plans, but we preferred to leave the problem of reconciling them for a later time. We talked instead about the political gossip of the moment or about what Alan García's next machination might be—what ambush, intrigue or infamy he might be preparing. Sometimes we did succeed in discussing—if we could manage to keep Belaúnde from wandering off—the question of whether the Alliance should present joint candidates in the municipal elections. The elections were set for November 1989, five months before the presidential election. Bedoya and I both felt that we should present joint candidates. Belaúnde disagreed. The subject would present us with our most serious crisis and came close to bringing about the end of the Alliance. It was in itself an education in politics.

On 29 October 1988, the three of us settled on a constitution —it took us a full year to draw it up—and it was agreed that we would present it in a ceremony in the Plaza de Armasin Trujillo. The presentation, however, served only to reveal the quarrels and rivalries between us. Contrary to what had been agreed on for public appearances—that everyone deliver the same cheers and slogans to show the 'fraternal spirit' that reigned in the alliance—supporters of each of the three parties hailed only its own leader and shouted only its own rallying cries, to show who was stronger.

At one rally there was an argument over the order of speakers. Bedoya insisted that as the leader and future presidential

Left to right: Luis Bedoya, Fernando Belaúnde and Mario Vargas Llosa on the day the Alliance was announced in April 1989.

Photo: J. Razuri

candidate, I ought to have top billing and deliver the closing address. Belaúnde objected on the grounds of his age and his status as ex-President. Belaúnde prevailed: I spoke first, then Bedoya, and Belaúnde ended the meeting. Matters of protocol took up much of our time and gave rise to suspicions and jealousies.

The realities of politics became particularly evident when finally we confronted the municipal elections. They would serve as the preliminary round of the presidential electoral contest and would be a measure of the relative strength of the contending parties. Before we had even properly discussed the subject, Belaúnde announced that Popular Action would put up its own candidates, since the Alliance existed only for the presidential election.

Bedoya agreed with me that if each of the three political forces went its separate way in these preliminary elections it would create an image of division and antagonism that would drastically reduce the chances of the Alliance taking root. When we were by ourselves, Belaúnde told me that the populist rank and file of his party wouldn't stand for the idea of sharing the candidates with the Christian Popular Party, which had little influence outside of Lima, and that he could not risk having rebellions within his party.

Since the whole problem was about a bid for the most power, I said that the *Libertad* movement would be prepared to abandon the idea of putting up any candidate for mayor or alderman or any other municipal office anywhere in Peru, so that Popular Action and the Christian Popular Party could share the candidacies between them. I thought that this gesture would make it easier for us to come to an agreement. But not even then would Belaúnde agree. The matter attracted the attention of the news media, which, biased in favour of the government, did their utmost to show the internal weakness and tension that, according to them, were eating away at our alliance.

Finally, after innumerable arguments—some so heated they seemed on the verge of becoming violent—Belaúnde gave in and accepted my proposal. Another fight began between Popular Action and the Christian Popular Party, this time over which of the two would put up the candidate for each of the municipalities. They never reached an agreement; neither party seemed prepared to make further concessions. In the meanwhile, members of the *Libertad* movement objected to the agreement I had made with Belaúnde and Bedoya—not to put up municipal candidates ourselves—and there were a number of defections.

Belaúnde had placed the greatest obstacles in the way of an agreement concerning the municipal elections, but it was Bedoya who brought on the crisis. On the night of 19 June 1989, Bedoya appeared on television and denied what I had just announced at a press conference: that Popular Action and the Christian Popular Party had reached agreement over the municipal candidacies in Lima and Callao, the two most hotly disputed elections. I watched Bedoya's declaration just after getting into bed. I got up, went to my desk and spent the rest of the night reflecting on my difficult position and the disunity of the Alliance.

FRENTE DEMOCRATICO (THE ALLIANCE): *Libertad* (Mario Vargas Llosa), Popular Action (Fernando Belaúnde), Christian Popular Party (Luis Bedoya). Presidential candidate in 1990: Mario Vargas Llosa.

CHANGE '90: Presidential candidate in 1990: Alberto Fujimori.

APRA (AMERICAN POPULAR REVOLUTIONARY ALLIANCE) Leader: Alan García (President of Peru 1985–90). Presidential candidate in 1990: Luis Alva Castro.

UNITED LEFT: Presidential candidate in 1990: Henry Pease.

SOCIALIST LEFT: Presidential candidate in 1990: Alfonso Barrantes

Was it worthwhile to go on with the commitment I had made? Popular Action and the Christian Popular Party would continue squabbling to see who was going to head the electoral lists and how many aldermen and mayors each party would get until the Alliance had lost all its prestige. Was it in this spirit that we would achieve the great peaceful transformation of Peru? Was it possible with such an attitude to turn Peru into a 'country of owners and entrepreneurs', rid it of mercantilist practices, do away with the mentality of the hand-out and foster popular capitalism? If we were elected, would we do exactly as the Apristas had done—divide up the administration into small units and create more public posts for party loyalists?

I had been blind to what was going on. Had Belaúnde and Bedoya forgotten Peru? Whole regions—the Huallaga area, in the jungle, and almost all of the central Andes—were under the effective control of *Sendero Luminoso* and the Túpac Amaru Movement. Companies were working at a half and sometimes a third of their proven capacity. Tax revenues had fallen off, and the country was suffering from a general collapse of public services. Every night the television screens showed heart-breaking scenes of hospitals without medicines or beds, schools without desks and blackboards and sometimes without roofs or walls, districts without water or light, streets strewn with refuse, production workers and office clerks on strike to protest the dizzying fall in the standard of living. And the Alliance, born amid hopes of remedying this catastrophe, was paralyzed for weeks, months, over which party would propose its list in the municipalities!

Dawn came and I drew up a letter addressed to Belaúnde and Bedoya, informing them that, in view of their inability to reach an agreement, I was giving up my candidacy for president. I woke Patricia up to read her the text, and we made plans to go abroad to avoid the expected reaction. I had been invited to receive a literary prize in Italy, and the next day we bought our tickets, in secret, for twenty-four hours later. I sent the letter, via Alvaro, my elder son, to Belaúnde and Bedoya, after informing the executive committee of *Libertad* of my decision. My friends wore sad faces on receiving the news, but none of them attempted to dissuade me. They too were tired of the absurd way in which the Alliance had bogged down.

I gave instructions to the security guards not to allow anyone to enter the house, and we unplugged the telephone. The news reached the media and had the effect of an explosive. All the channels began their nightly news programme with the story. Reporters surrounded our house, and supplicants arrived from all the political camps of the Alliance. But I received no one and did not come out of the house when, later in the evening, hundreds of libertarians demonstrated outside.

Early in the morning of 22 June the security guards took us to the airport and got us aboard the Air France flight. We avoided another demonstration of libertarians, whom I spied in the distance from the window of the plane. When we arrived in Italy, two journalists were waiting for me. Heaven only knows how they had discovered I was coming. One was Juan Cruz from *El País* in Madrid, the other was Paul Yule of the BBC, who was making a documentary on my candidacy: he was the first to express the view that my withdrawal had simply been a tactic to force my intractable allies to give in.

In fact most people ultimately viewed my withdrawal as proof that I wasn't such a bad politician after all. The truth is that it was not planned, but was a genuine expression of my loathing for the political manoeuvring in which I found myself submerged. This is disputed by Patricia, who lets me get away with nothing. I did not, she says, announce that my resignation was irrevocable, and she thinks that in some secret place I harboured the illusion, the desire, that my letter would settle the differences among the allies.

It certainly appeared to have that effect. On the day I left, the independent media began to criticize Bedoya and Belaúnde severely. The number of people who were prepared to vote for me rose markedly. The opinion polls had always shown me to be the leading candidate, but I never had support greater than thirty-five per cent. After my withdrawal that figure rose to fifty per cent, the highest I attained at any point in the campaign. In my absence *Libertad* enrolled thousands of new members, ran out of membership cards and had to print new ones. Local headquarters were filled to overflowing, day and night, by supporters who wanted *Libertad* to break with Popular Action and the Christian Popular Party and go before the voters by itself. I learned later that 4,980 letters had arrived from all over Peru, congratulating me for having broken with the two parties, with Popular Action in particular.

Mark Malloch Brown managed to reach me to congratulate me as well. He was a member of the public relations firm Sawyer Miller—we had only recently hired their services—and he had already advised me before to break with the allies. He wanted me to present myself as an independent candidate coming to 'save' Peru from the state in which the 'politicians' had plunged it. His surveys, he said, had shown that there was, in the heart of the country, a profound disillusionment with, if not outright contempt for, political parties, particularly those that had already enjoyed power.

He was, therefore, delighted to learn of my resignation and was not in the least surprised by the instant shift of public opinion in my favour. He thought I had planned it all.

Mark once said to me that I was the worst candidate he had ever worked with.

Patricia and I took refuge in the south of Spain, still fleeing from the press. I had decided to stick with my withdrawal. I had a long-standing offer to spend a year in Berlin, and I proposed to Patricia that we go there.

The news then reached me that Popular Action and the Christian Popular Party had reached agreement on all points of contention between them and had drawn up joint lists of candidates for all municipal contests. Their differences had vanished, as if by magic. They were waiting for me to return to Peru, to rejoin the Alliance and resume my campaign.

My first reaction was to say to myself: 'I'm not coming. I'm no good at that sort of thing. I don't know how to carry it off, and what's more, I don't like it. These months have given me more than enough time to realize that. I'll stick to my books and my papers, which I never should have left.' My wife and I had another argument, one of the longest and loudest of our married life. She, who had come close to threatening to divorce me if I became a candidate, now urged me to go back to Peru, marshalling moral and patriotic arguments. Since Belaúnde and Bedoya had backed down, there was no alternative. That had been the reason for my resignation, hadn't it? Well then, it no longer existed. Too many good, unselfish, decent people back in Peru were working day and night for the Alliance. They had believed my speeches and exhortations. Was I going to let them down, now that Popular Action and the Christian Popular Party were beginning to behave decently? The sawtooth mountain ranges of the lovely Andalusian town of Mijas echo to her admonitions: 'We've taken on a responsibility. We have to go back.'

That is what we did. I reconfirmed my candidacy for the president of the Republic of Peru.

6

One night, a man from Los Jazmines, the slum adjoining the airport of Pucallpa, saw two men emerging out of a patch of underbrush who then proceeded towards the end of the runway. They stopped—one of two unscheduled *Aero-Perú* flights had just arrived from Lima—and then turned back. They were carrying something. The man from Los Jazmines alerted other people from the slum, who formed a patrol armed with clubs and machetes, and went to the runway to check on the two men. They found, surrounded and apprehended them, but as they were about to take them to the police station, the two men drew revolvers and fired point-blank. A man named Sergio Pasavi was shot six times in the stomach—his intestines were perforated. A man named José Vásquez was shot in the leg, his thigh-bone shattered. Humberto Jacobo, a barber, was shot in the shoulder, his collar-bone fractured. Víctor Ravello Cruz was shot in the groin. The two strangers then got away but they left a bomb behind, a two-kilo 'Russian cheese', containing dynamite, aluminium, nails, buckshot, bits of metal and a short wick. They were intending to throw the bomb at the second unscheduled flight from Lima, a small Fawcett twin-engine plane, that, having left at the same time as the *Aero-Perú* flight, was two hours late. I was on that plane.

Shortly after the municipal elections on 26 November 1989, a naval officer, dressed in civilian clothes and obviously taking unusual precautions, arrived at my house. A meeting between us had been arranged in person by a mutual friend, Jorge Salmón, since my telephones had been bugged. The officer arrived in a car with protective glass windows. He had come to tell me that the Office of Naval Intelligence, to which he belonged, had learned of a secret meeting held in the National Museum, attended by President Alan García; his minister of the interior, Augustín Mantilla, who was widely held to be the organizer of the counter-terrorist gangs; Carlos Roca, a congressman; and Kitazona, the head of security, García's 'élite' paratroopers. At this meeting it had been decided to eliminate me, along with my son and two

Photo: Julio Etchart

FRED
FREDEMO

other political colleagues. The assassinations would take place in a way that would suggest that it was the work of *Sendero Luminoso*.

The officer presented me with a report that the intelligence service had forwarded to the Chief Commandant of the Navy. I asked him how seriously the service regarded this report. He shrugged and said that if the river made a noise it was carrying stones, as the saying had it. My son Alvaro passed the news to Jaime Bayle, a young television reporter, who made it public. The Navy denied the report's existence.

Less than a month later, *Acción Solidaria*, a group sponsored by *Libertad* and headed by Patricia, organized a rally in the Alianza Lima Stadium, with the participation of film, radio and television celebrities. It was attended by 35,000 people. Shortly after the rally began, it was announced over the radio that a bomb had been found in my house and that the bomb squad of the Civil Guard had managed to defuse it. My mother and in-laws, the secretaries and the assistants, were forced to leave the house. That the bomb was discovered as the rally was beginning suggested that the perpetrators had intended to spoil the celebration and make us leave. Patricia and my children and I decided to remain until the rally ended. The suspicion that it was not a real bomb attempt but a ploy was confirmed that night, when the bomb squad of the Civil Guard assured us that the 'device'—discovered by the watchman of a tourism school next door—wasn't filled with dynamite but with sand.

There were always meant to be attempts on my life and the lives of my family. Some were so absurd that they made us laugh. Others were obvious fabrications of the informants who used them as pretexts to get through to me. Still others, like the anonymous telephone calls, appeared to be psychological manoeuvres by Alan García's followers, intended to demoralize us. And then there were the reports by 'people of good will', who in reality knew nothing precise, but suspected that I might be killed and came to talk to me about vague ambushes and mysterious attempts on my life because that was their way of begging me to take care. In the final stage of the campaign this reached such proportions that it became necessary to put a stop to it. I asked Patricia and my secretaries not to grant appointments to anyone who had asked to discuss 'a serious and secret subject having to do with the Doctor's security' (in Peru I'm called 'Doctor').

Was I afraid? Apprehensive, yes, many times, but more of objects that I could see being hurled at me than of bullets or bombs. One tense night in Casma, as I was going up to the speakers' platform, Aprista counter-demonstrators bombarded us with stones and eggs. Patricia was hit on the forehead with an egg. In Lima one morning, the good head (in all senses) of my friend Enrique Ghersi, who was walking beside me, stopped the stone that had been hurled at me (I got away with being doused in smelly red paint).

My life had changed. It ceased to be private. Until I left Peru in June 1990, after the second round of voting for the presidency, I lost the privacy that I had always guarded jealously.

At all hours people were at my house, holding meetings, conducting interviews, organizing demonstrations, talking with me, Patricia or my son Alvaro (who would eventually become our press spokesman). Reception rooms, hallways, stairways were occupied by men and women whom I had never met. I often didn't know what they were doing there. I was reminded of Carlos Germán Belli's poem: 'This is not your house.'

A room was built next to my study, where I always wrote by hand, to hold new machinery: computers, faxes, photocopy machines, intercoms, typewriters, new telephone lines, filing cabinets. This new office, only a few steps from our bedroom, operated from early in the morning till late at night, except during the weeks immediately preceding the election, when it operated until dawn. I came to feel that I was living on permanent exhibition, that every intimate detail of my life had become public information.

For a time we had two bodyguards inside the house. Armed men with pistols appeared wherever I turned and terrified my mother and mother-in-law, until finally Patricia ordered them to stay outside the house.

The campaign forced me to give up my favourite afternoon activity: wandering through different neighbourhoods, exploring the streets, slipping into matinées at local movie houses that creak with old people and where the fleas make viewing impossible, climbing on to jitneys and public buses with no fixed destination, learning little by little the secrets of the labyrinth that is Lima. In recent years I had become well-known in Peru—more for my television programme than for my books—and it was no longer easy for me to stroll about anonymously. But now it was impossible. I could not go anywhere without being surrounded by people and applauded or booed. Being followed by reporters and surrounded by bodyguards—after the first two bodyguards, there were then four, then in the last months fifteen or so—made for a spectacle that looked like something between a clown's act and a provocative display of aggression. My schedule left me with little time for things unrelated to politics, but even in my rare free moments it was unthinkable for me to enter a book shop. My public appearances gave rise to demonstrations, as happened at a recital by Alicia Maguiña in the Teatro Municipal, where the audience, on seeing me come in with Patricia, divided into supporters who applauded and opponents who stamped on the floor and jeered. In order to see José Sanchis Sinisterra's play, *Ay, Carmela*, without incident, I sat by myself, in the balcony of the Open Air Theatre. I mention these performances because they were the only ones I attended during my campaign. As for movies, which I am as fond of as I am of books and the theatre, I went two or three times at most, but I was always forced to attend them in the manner of someone who had sneaked in (entering after the film began and leaving before it ended). The last time I attended the cinema—the Cine San Antonio in the Miraflores district of Lima—I was forced to leave early: halfway through, one of my colleagues found my seat and told me that one of our headquarters had been bombed and that the watchman had been shot. I went to soccer games two or three times and to a volleyball match, as well as to bullfights, but these appearances had been decided on by the campaign directors of the Alliance, for the purpose of 'mingling with the crowd'.

There were a few diversions that Patricia and I could allow ourselves. One was going to the houses of friends for dinner. Another was eating in a restaurant, although when we were there we felt like performers in a stage show. I often thought, my spine tingling: 'I've lost my freedom.' If I were president, my life would continue like this for five more years. And I remember the odd feeling—it was happiness—when, on 14 June 1990, I landed in Paris—it was all over at last—and before unpacking I went for a walk down the Boulevard Saint-Germain. I was a free man once again. I was an anonymous passer-by. I was without escorts or police bodyguards. I was not recognized. And then, all of a sudden, as if by spontaneous generation, there appeared in front of me, blocking my way, the ubiquitous, omniscient Juan Cruz, of *El País*, to whom I found it impossible to deny an interview.

When my political life began, I resolved: 'I'm not going to stop reading and writing for at least a few hours every day. Not even if I become president.' It wasn't a selfish decision. It was dictated by my conviction that what I wanted to do, as a candidate and as head of state, would be done better—with greater will, enthusiasm and imagination—if I kept intact a private, personal space of ideas, reflections, dreams and intellectual work, walled in to keep out politics and current events.

I fulfilled only part of my promise: I read, although not as much as I had hoped. Writing was impossible. It wasn't only for lack of time. Although I woke very early, and entered my study before the secretaries arrived, I never got used to the idea that I was actually alone. It was as if some mysterious muse, unknown to me until then, had grown resentful at the lack of solitude and had left my study for good. It was impossible for me to concentrate, to give myself over to the play of imagination, to attain that state of breaking away complctely from and suspending everything around me, which is what is so marvellous about writing fiction and, in my case, essential to be able to do it. Preoccupations far removed from pure literature kept interfering, and there was no way of banishing them, of escaping from the march of events. In the three years of my campaign I wrote only a series of forewords for a collection of modern novels, and some speeches, articles and little essays on politics.

With so little time, I became very exacting in my reading. I stayed on safe ground: I couldn't offer myself the luxury of reading as widely or anarchically as had been my habit. I chose books that I knew would hypnotize me. I re-read Malraux's *La condition humaine*, Melville's *Moby-Dick*, Faulkner's *Light in August* and Borges's short stories. So little intelligence was involved in my daily round of political tasks that I was eager to read difficult works of philosophy and social thought. I began to study the works of Karl Popper, whose *The Open Society and its Enemies* had come to my attention in 1980. Every day, early in the morning, before going out for my daily run, when it was barely daylight and the quiet of the house reminded me of the pre-political period of my life, I read Popper.

At night, before going to sleep, I read poetry—always the classics of the Spanish Golden Age, and usually Góngora. It was a purifying bath. I stepped away from arguments, plots, intrigues, invectives, and was welcomed into a perfect world, resplendently harmonious, inhabited by nymphs and villains, full of coded references to Greek and Roman fictions, of subtle music and bare, spare architectures. I had read Góngora since my university years with a rather distant admiration; his perfection seemed to me a touch inhuman and his world too cerebral and chimerical. But now I was grateful to him for being abstract and remote, for having built a Baroque enclave outside of time, suspended in an illustrious realm of intellect and sensibility, emancipated from the ugly, the mean and petty, the mediocre, from the sordid facts of daily life.

Between the first and second rounds of the election, I was unable even to do my morning reading, although I tried, sitting down in my study with Popper's *Conjectures and Refutations* or *Objective Knowledge* in my hands. I was preoccupied with the campaign, with the news of murders and of attempts on people's lives—over a hundred people, many with ties to *Libertad*, were assassinated in a two-month period. I had to give up my morning reading. But not a single night, not even the night of the election, went by without my reading a sonnet of Góngora's, or a strophe of his *Polifemo* or his *Soledades*, or one of his ballads or rondelets; and through these verses, my life became purer, even though it was only for a few minutes.

Allow me to put on record my enduring gratitude to the great Cordovan poet.

7

Campaigning in the Andes was difficult. To avoid being ambushed, we had to move suddenly and unexpectedly, with a small party, sending someone in advance to alert the most reliable people at our destination that we would be arriving in one or two days' time. It was impossible to go overland to many provinces of the central mountain region—Juníin had become, after Ayacucho, the *departamento* victimized by the most attacks. The journey had to be made in small planes that landed in unimaginable places—cemeteries, soccer fields, river beds—or in light helicopters which, if a storm suddenly overtook us, had to set down wherever they could—on top of a mountain sometimes—until the weather cleared. These acrobatics completely unnerved some of my colleagues. Beatriz Merino took out crosses, rosaries and holy images she wore over her heart and invoked the protection of the saints at the top of her voice. Pedro Cateriano intimidated the pilots into giving him reassuring explanations about the flight instruments and kept pointing out the threatening thunderheads, the sharp peaks that suddenly loomed up or the snaky rays of lightning that zigzagged all about us.

The central Andes had been subjected constantly to terrorism and counter-terrorism. One by one, roads were disappearing because no one maintained them or because the *Sendero Luminoso* had blown up the bridges with dynamite and blocked the trails so as to stop all traffic. *Sendero Luminoso* had also destroyed crops and livestock, wrecked buildings and killed off hundreds of vicuñas that used to graze on the reserve of Pampa Galeras and pillaged agricultural co-operatives—

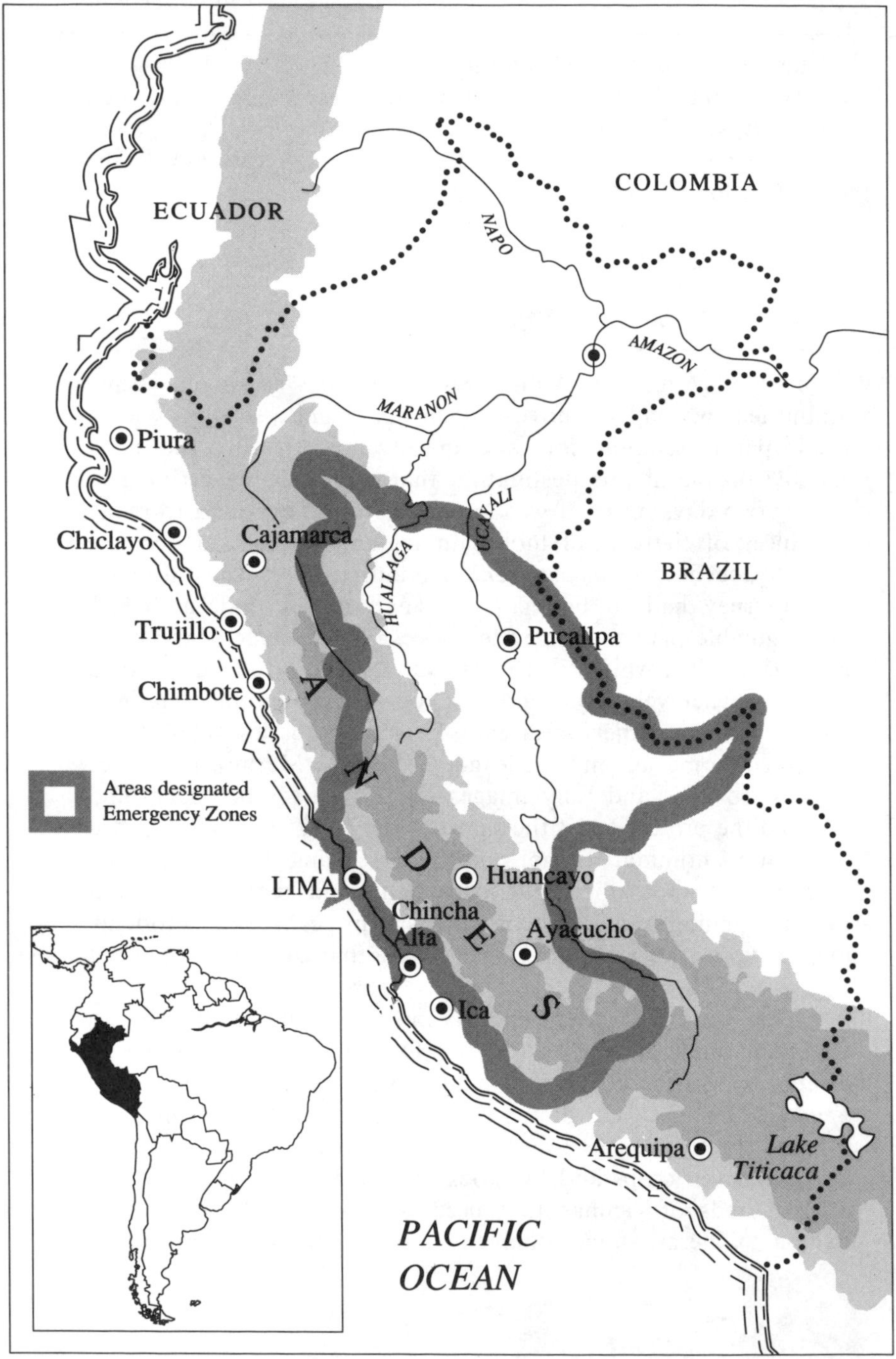

ECUADOR
COLOMBIA
NAPO
AMAZON
MARANON
BRAZIL
UCAYALI
HUALLAGA
Piura
Chiclayo
Cajamarca
Trujillo
Pucallpa
Chimbote
A N D E S
Areas designated Emergency Zones
LIMA
Huancayo
Chincha Alta
Ayacucho
Ica
Arequipa
Lake Titicaca
PACIFIC OCEAN

principally those of the Valle de Mantaro, the most dynamic in the high country. *Sendero Luminoso* had assassinated agents from the ministry of agriculture and foreign experts in rural development. It had murdered small-scale farmers and miners, blown up tractors, power plants and hydro-electric installations. It had killed the cattle and it had killed members of the co-operatives and communes who opposed *Sendero Luminoso*'s scorched-earth policy, which was intended to throttle the cities to death, Lima above all, by allowing no food to reach them.

Words are inadequate. Expressions such as 'subsistence economy' or 'critical poverty' do not convey the extent of human suffering, the impoverishment of the environment, the utter lack of hope. Entire families were fleeing these Andean villages, their walls daubed with the hammer and sickle and the slogans of the *Sendero Luminoso*, abandoning everything, driven half mad with desperation because of the violence and poverty. They were heading, armies of unemployed, for our 'new towns'—slums, shanty settlements on the outskirts of the cities—swelling them, overcrowding them, as though survivors of some Biblical catastrophe. I often thought: 'A country can always be worse off. Underdevelopment is bottomless.'

I remember the young, little soldier, practically a child, whom they brought to me at the abandoned airport of Jauja, on 8 September 1989, so that we could take him back to Lima with us. He had survived an attack that noon in which two of his friends had died—we had heard the bombs and the shots from the platform where we were holding our rally—and he was now losing a lot of blood. We made room for him in the small plane by asking one of the bodyguards to stay behind. The boy was obviously under the army's minimum age of eighteen. He was holding a container of serum up above him, but his strength gave out, and we took turns holding it up. He didn't complain once during the flight. He stared blankly into space, with an astounded, wordless desperation, as though trying to understand what had happened to him.

I remember how, on 14 February 1990, as we were leaving the Milpa mine in Cerro de Pasco, the triple glass windscreen of our light truck shattered, turning into a spiderweb at the height of my temple, just as we were driving past a hostile group. 'This was supposed to be an armoured truck,' the head of the campaign protested.

'It is,' he was assured, 'against bullets. But that was a stone.' It wasn't protected against cudgels either, because a few weeks before, in Cayaltí, outside a sugar mill, a group of Apristas had smashed all our windows.

There were the committee members of Cerro de Pasco who turned up at a regional meeting. Some were battered and bruised, and others were wounded—that morning a terrorist commando unit had attacked their headquarters. And there were the members of the committee of Ayacucho, the centre of the *Sendero Luminoso* rebellion, where human life was worth less than anywhere else in Peru. Every time I went to Ayacucho—I made the trip a number of times—and met with the committee chairman Oscar Terrones, I was assailed by guilt: I felt that I was in the presence of men and women who might die at any moment. When we agreed on the candidates for national and regional elections, we knew that the men and women of Ayacucho were in especial danger. We offered to hide them until after the election, but they did not take up the offer. Instead, they asked me if I could persuade the military head of the region to allow them to go about armed. He refused me permission. Shortly before my meeting with the military head, there had been an incident: our candidate for a seat in the regional legislature, Julián Huamaní Yauri, had heard people climbing up on to the roof of his house and ran out into the street. The second time, on 4 March 1990, he did not have time to get out. They surprised him at his front door, in broad daylight, and after gunning him down, the killers walked off calmly through a crowd which ten years of terror had taught not to see, hear or lift a finger in protest. I remember the badly mangled body of Julián Huamaní Yauri in his coffin, on that sunny morning in Ayacucho and the weeping of his wife and his mother, a peasant woman who, with her arms around me, sobbed out words in Quechua that I couldn't understand.

Photo: J. Razuri

8

The philosopher Francisco Miró Quesada, an old friend and an experienced politician, visited regularly and wrote me long letters of advice. He had been one of the leaders of Popular Action. He was very unhopeful. No political party in Peru, he had concluded, had been able to sustain a democratic structure. 'It doesn't matter if the parties are of the right or the left,' he said, 'they fill up with scoundrels.' *Libertad* did not fill up with scoundrels, but it never became the modern, popular, democratic institution that I dreamed of. From the start it contracted the vices of Peruvian political parties: cliques, factionalism and caciques—that special breed of Peruvian political bosses. There were groups that took over committees and encysted themselves inside, becoming closed circles that kept others from participating. Or there were groups paralyzed by internal squabbles over trivial matters, which drove away valuable people who, although they sympathized with our ideas, did not care to waste their time in intrigues and petty rivalries.

There were exceptions as in Arequipa, where the organizing group, a tightly knit team of young men and women, managed to create an efficient infrastructure. Others, such as La Libertad, were perhaps more typical. There the initial group split into two factions. Then it split into three factions. And then for three whole years they fought among themselves over the leadership. The membership naturally never increased. And there were several, such as the group in Puno, where we made the mistake of entrusting the organization to unreliable people without ability. I will not forget the impression it made on me to note, on a visit to the communities of the altiplano, that our *departamento* secretary treated the peasants with the same arrogance as did the old-time political bosses.

We accepted, I now see, offers of help from people whom we never screened. Sometimes we were lucky and made precisely the right choice; at other times, we made monumental errors. The errors should have been corrected. We failed to correct them and in many places the movement was born crooked, and

Bienvenidos

it later proved difficult to twist back into the proper shape. I was aware of what was going to happen but I could do nothing about it. My admonitions, whether plaintive or enraged, in the executive and political committees, that the leaders must go out into the provinces, had little effect. They were happy to travel with me to appear at demonstrations, but lightning campaign visits did not further the work of organization. I told them that their inclination towards the sedentary life would have regrettable consequences. And that was how it turned out. With a few exceptions the organization of *Libertad* in the interior proved to be far from representative and far from democratic. In our committees as well there reigned and fulminated that immortal figure: the cacique.

I met many of these caciques: they might be from the coast, or the mountains, or the jungle; they were all cut from the same cloth by the same tailor. They were or had been or inevitably would become: senators, congressmen, mayors, prefects, sub-prefects. Their energy, their abilities, their Machiavellian machinations and their imagination were all concentrated on just one goal: to attain, hang on to or recover a modicum of power through every means, licit or illicit, at their disposal. They were all ardent followers of the moral philosophy that a Peruvian politician summed up in the words: 'To live without your expenses accounted for in the annual budget is to live in error.' All of them had a little court or retinue of relatives, friends and protégés whom they made out to be popular leaders—of teachers, of peasants, of workers, of technicians—and placed them on the committees they presided over. They had all changed ideologies and parties the way one changes one's shirt, and they had all been or at some point would be Apristas, populists and communists. They were always there, waiting for me, on the roads, in the stations, at the airports, with bouquets of flowers and bands and bags of herbs to throw for good luck, and theirs were the first arms to reach out and hug me wherever I arrived, with the same boundless love with which they had embraced General Velasco, Belaúnde, Barrantes, Alan García, and they always managed things in such a way as to be at my side on the speakers' platform, microphone in hand, introducing me to those present and offering to organize rallies and doing everything possible to be seen with me in the newspapers and on television. They were always the ones who, when a demonstration was over, tried to carry me about in triumph on their shoulders—a ridiculous custom of Peruvian politicians in imitation of bullfighters, and one that I always refused to allow, even if I occasionally had to defend myself with a good swift kick—and they were the ones who sponsored the inevitable receptions, banquets, dinners, lunches, barbecues, which they made into even grander occasions by giving flowery speeches. Usually they were attorneys, but among them there were also owners of garages or transportation companies, or former policemen or ex-members of the armed forces, and I would even go so far as to swear that they all looked alike, with their tight suits, their little *de rigeur* moustaches and their thunderous, saccharine, high-flown eloquence, ready to rain down in torrents at the slightest opportunity.

I remember one in his fifties, a perfect specimen, in Tumbes. He was bald and had a cheerful smile—a gold tooth. He was introduced to me on the first political junket I made to the region in December 1987. He climbed out of a car that was belching smoke, with an entourage of half a dozen people whom he defined in these words: 'The pioneers of *Libertad*, Doctor. And I, sir, am the helmsman, at your service.' I found out later that at one time he had been a 'helmsman' of Apra, and after that of Popular Action, a party he deserted in order to serve the dictatorship. And after going through our ranks, he contrived to become a leader of Francisco Díez Canseco's Independent Civic Union, and finally, of our ally the SODE, which put him up as a regional candidate of the Alliance.

Battling with caciques, tolerating caciques, using caciques was something I never learned how to do. I am certain that these caciques saw on my face the disgust and the impatience they aroused in me, representing as they did, at the provincial level, everything that I would have liked politics in Peru *not* to be: something dirty, venal and amoral. But this did not prevent the committees of *Libertad* in the provinces from falling into the

wrong hands. How to change something so visceral, that was such an integral component of our political nature? And what effects would it have on the government in days to come?

I had believed that it would have been possible to find in the provinces an independent organizing group without a political past but with the kind of civic and professional prestige that would attract local popular support. And I believed that, once a fair number of people of this kind signed up, elections could be held within the movement from which true leaders would emerge. In Arequipa, in Piura and in a few other places that is how things turned out. But in many localities it was the caciques who constituted the organizing group and who called for the elections—after holding out against them as long as they could—that were then frequently suspect. It had always been like this in Peru. But that it should also be like this, in a movement committed to cleaning up our democratic system, was disturbing.

Peru is an 'old country', as the novelist José María Arguedas has said, and nothing betrays how far back in time the Peruvian psyche goes as the people's love of ceremony. Wherever I went there was always a brightly decorated speaker's platform, with flowers, flags and paper garlands hanging from the walls and ceilings, and a table with things to eat and drink after the official ritual. There was a group of musicians and sometimes folk dancers from the mountains or the coast. The parish priest never failed to show up, to sprinkle holy water about and bless the local headquarters (which might be nothing more than a crude structure made of cane and rush-matting). The members of the crowd would be dressed in vivid colours, wearing their very best clothes, the ones kept for a wedding or a baptism. At the beginning and at the end we sung the theme song of *Libertad.* And in between there were a great many speeches, as every last member of the local board—the general secretary, the secretary of culture, the secretary of sports, the secretary of official records, the secretary of the economy, the secretary of women's activities, the secretary of programmes for young people, the secretary of government planning—had to speak: no one was to feel left out. The ceremony went on—and on and on

And afterwards a document in baroque legalese, with many great seals, had to be signed, bearing witness to the fact that the ceremony had taken place, anointing it and sanctifying it. And *then* came the show: folk music, *huaynitos* from the high country, *marineras* from Trujillo, black dances from Chincha, *pasillos* from Piura. And although I begged, ordered, pleaded—explaining that with such grand and glorious activities the whole campaign schedule went to hell—I seldom managed to get them to make these ceremonies any shorter, or to allow me to slip off from the picture-taking and the autograph sessions, or to get out of being the target of handfuls of '*pica-pica*', a demoniacal powder that worked its way all over one's body and into the most hidden recesses and itched like crazy.

Amid all this, did ideas matter? I persisted in the belief that they did; I persisted in speaking. I improvised and delivered hundreds of speeches. I spoke several times each day, morning and night, and in the last weeks before the elections there were three or four rallies a day. To keep my throat in good condition, Bedoya advised me to chew whole cloves between one speech and the next, and the physician who accompanied me—there were two or three of them, who took turns, along with a small emergency team in case there was an attempt on my life—kept stuffing lozenges down my gullet and handing me throat spray. I tried not to talk between meetings, to give my throat every possible chance to recuperate, but even so I was speaking so much it was sometimes impossible to keep my voice from turning hoarse or my throat from clogging up with phlegm.

Speaking in public squares was something I had never done—classes and lectures are no help. In Peru a politician doesn't go up on to the platform to speak; he has to put on a show. His aim is to charm, to seduce, to lull, to bill and to coo. His musical phrasing is more important than his ideas, his gestures more important than his concepts. Form is everything. The good orator may say absolutely nothing, but he says it well. What matters to his audience is that he sounds good and looks good. Logic, or rational order, or consistency, get in the way of his achieving his effect, which is attained above all through impressionistic images and metaphors, ham acting, fancy turns of phrase and defiant remarks. The good Latin-American political orator bears a much closer resemblance to a bullfighter or a rock singer than to a lecturer or a professor: he communicates with his audience by instinct, emotion and sentiment.

Michel Leiris has compared the art of writing to bullfighting, suggested by the risk a poet or prose writer is prepared to accept when confronting the blank page. But the analogy is more appropriate for the politician who, from atop a few boards, on a balcony or in the atrium of a church, faces a crowd worked up to fever pitch. He has before him something as massive as a bull, a fearful creature and yet one so ingenuous and manipulable that it can be made to move in any direction—provided the politician knows how to handle the red cape of intonation and gesture with dexterity.

During my first speech, that night in the Plaza San Martín, which seems like so many years ago, I was surprised to discover how unsteady and precarious the attention of a crowd was and how elementary was its psychology. I was surprised by the ease with which a crowd can be made to pass from laughter to anger, or be moved, or driven into a frenzy, or reduced to tears. And I was also surprised by how difficult it was to reason with a crowd, rather than engage its passions. The language of politics has always been made up of platitudes; in a culture with a centuries-old custom demanding that public speaking be an incantatory art, the platitudes abound.

I did not want to perpetuate that custom. I wanted to use speaker's platforms to promote ideas, reveal the programme of the Alliance and avoid demagoguery and clichés. To my way of thinking, the plaza represented the ideal place to put across the view that voting for me was voting for reform.

To what extent did we manage to make *ideas* put down roots among libertarians? To what extent did the Peruvians who voted for me vote for liberal ideas? I don't know. These are doubts that I would like very much to clear up, since they hold the key to whether the effort of these years was useless or worthwhile.

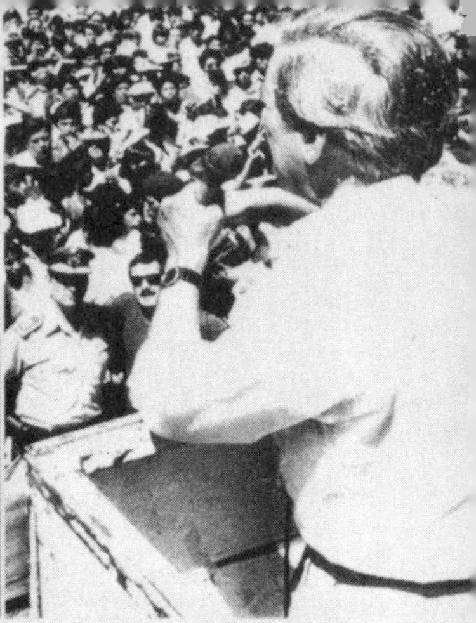

I had already seen that ideas mattered little in my endless meetings with Belaúnde and Bedoya. Those meetings confirmed for me something that I had already suspected: that real politics, not the kind that one reads and writes and thinks about—the only sort that I had been acquainted with—but the politics that is lived and practised day by day, has little to do with ideas, values and imagination, with long-range visions, with notions of an ideal society, with generosity, solidarity or idealism. It consists almost exclusively of manoeuvres, intrigues, plots, pacts, paranoias, betrayals, a great deal of calculation, no little cynicism and every variety of con game. What really gets professional politicians moving, whether of the centre, the left or the right, what excites them and drives them on, is *power*: attaining it, remaining in it or returning to it as soon as possible. There are exceptions, of course, but they are just that: exceptions. Many politicians begin their careers impelled by altruistic sentiments, by the desire to change society, promote justice, improve the standard of living. But along the way, in the petty, pedestrian practise that politics is, the fine objectives cease to exist, become mere commonplaces of speeches and programmes. Anyone who is not capable of feeling the obsessive, almost physical attraction to power finds it nearly impossible to be a successful politician.

No, finally, I don't believe that I succeeded in putting across what I wanted to. Peruvians did not vote for *ideas* in the elections. In the two months of the campaign for the second round, I tried to sum up our proposed programme in just a few ideas, which I repeated on my endless rounds of the new towns, again and again, in the most simple and direct way, enveloped in familiar popular imagery. But it did no good: the weekly polls always showed that the candidate who was attracting voters was doing so on the basis of his personality or out of some mysterious impulse: *never* on account of the programme on offer.

Of all the speeches I gave, I believe my best ones—or my least bad ones—were two that I was able to prepare in the hospitable garden of my two friends, Maggie and Carlos. I had no bodyguards, reporters or telephones. The first of these two speeches launched my candidacy, in the Plaza de Armas of Arequipa, on 4 June 1989, and the second closed the campaign, in the Paseo de la República, in Lima, on 4 April. It was the most personal one of all. And there was also, perhaps, one more. It was the brief address, written beforehand with my friends in mind, the people who had worked so hard with me on the campaign. I gave it on the afternoon of 10 June before the growing crowd that had rushed through the doors of the *Libertad* headquarters as soon as it became known that we had lost the election.

A democracy, I said, is driven by the electoral process, and in elections there are victories and defeats. But the work that had been done by the members of *Libertad* cannot be judged in this way. 'I know,' I said,

> I am certain, that Peru too will come to know and acknowledge this. That the seeds that we have sown together during these two and a half years will continue to germinate and finally produce those fruits that we desire for Peru: the fruits of modernity, justice, prosperity, peace and *libertad.*

It was my last political speech.

'Do you still remember,' Patricia said to me, as we were leaving, 'that you were once a writer?'

Translated from the Spanish by Helen Lane

Overleaf: Alberto Fujimori and Mario Vargas Llosa

SANTA ROSA
STAR

GRANTA

Alvaro Vargas Llosa

The Press Officer

Fourth of June 1989: thus, in a packed town square, Mario Vargas Llosa was proclaimed candidate for the presidency of the republic in the town of his birth, Arequipa.

A short time later my father came to London, a visit made at the suggestion of Adrian Beamish, the British ambassador in Lima, who thought it would give my father the chance to establish contact with members of the British government.

Octavio Paz was in London at the time, and my father arranged to meet him. I had assumed that I would be accompanying my father, but strangely, he told me that I was to remain behind. He had sensed that the meeting was not going to be an easy one. And it wasn't. Octavio spent the evening telling my father that, although his bravery was admirable, the sacrifice he was about to make would be infinitely regretted later. He spoke about the tradition of failure among intellectuals who had devoted themselves to politics, but in my father's case the prospect was more serious because he was too valuable a novelist to abandon literature. 'You're our leading novelist,' he told him in a moment of high emotion. Octavio also said that the limited mandate of a presidential term was too short to be able to do anything significant in a country as monstrously difficult as his own. 'The thing is that you're a progressive,' he joked. 'You believe in method.' Then, just before they parted, Octavio assured him: 'The best thing that can happen, Mario, is for you to lose.'

My father told him that the situation in Peru was more serious than could be imagined—so serious that a general civil war could break out, that the Apristas could remain in power indefinitely or that the state might fall into the hands of the communists.

Even so, my father was not at his ease. Octavio's words reminded my father of all his early doubts, doubts which now, in full political flight, he had to consign to oblivion.

A few hours later my father was informed that the British Prime Minister wished to receive him. I remember my own strong feelings: 'Tell her that your son is unable to admire her enough.'

Maggie, as always, came straight to the point once the

photo-session was over. The issue was the candidate's personal security. When so much is concentrated into a single person, she warned him, the most important thing is protection. In eliminating you, your enemies will have achieved a great deal.

'Are you well protected?' she asked, in a tone which implied that he would never be protected enough.

The conversation moved on to other topics. The Prime Minister reflected on her own early difficulties—the marches, the strikes, the protests, the people around her losing faith in their own ideas and in themselves.

The question that decides everything, she said, is: 'Do you hold back or do you press on? But if you hold back it's almost impossible to pick up where you left off until later on: the reforms will be lost. But if you continue you will have to endure a great deal of loneliness.' In order to survive those first traumatic months, Thatcher advised, it is indispensable to surround yourself with a selected group of people who think as you do. This was, acording to her, the secret of her success: having surrounded herself in 1979 with a first-class political guard, devoted to her ideas and capable of dealing with adversity. Her watchword: surround yourself with Thatcherites.

My father and Mrs Thatcher discussed other things: co-operation between Great Britain and Latin America; the need to transcend the enmity of the Falklands conflict. My father expressed his admiration for her reforms—he had witnessed many at first hand—and listened to her advice on the question of privatization, particularly concerning shareholders, who would form the backbone of our plan for government.

September 1989: the campaign began, properly speaking, when we set up the professional team designed to achieve the great objective: victory in the primaries. Like everyone else we were new to the game, and needed technical advice.

Our original intention had been to win the help of the English agency Saatchi and Saatchi, and we went to see them during my father's visit. They showed us the campaigns they had carried out on behalf of Margaret Thatcher, but after a few hours confessed that they didn't have time to go to Peru: they had just signed a contract with Hernan Buchi in Chile, and had embarked on a campaign designed to persuade the British electorate to oppose the EEC in its efforts to integrate the economies of the European governments.

We had also been approached by Sawyer Miller, but we hesitated before contracting a North American company, assuming that it would rely on highly emotive images rather than ideas. We did not want to win an election with a sensationalist campaign. To our surprise, however, the gringos from Sawyer Miller turned out to share our temperament. They had succeeded with Corazon Aquino's campaign in the Philippines, the 'No' campaign in Chile, Sanchez de Losada in Bolivia (although, for reasons of parliamentary arithmetics, he did not win the presidency) and Virgilio Barco in Colombia. Moreover, the representative of the Sawyer Miller team turned out to be English, Mark Malloch Brown. He directed the first survey of public opinion that defined our election strategy.

The key to his work lay in preparing studies of the electoral market by means of minute and exhaustive surveys, X-raying the behaviour of the population so that we could adjust our plans with the changes that occurred in the soul of the people. At no point did we act in a way that conflicted with our own convictions, and on dozens of occasions our own impulses led the campaign along twists and turns far from the pre-established plan. There were, as there had to be, moments of great tension.

Fifth of March 1990: as the date of the election approached, the violence spread. And then we heard the distressing news that Julián Huamaní Yauri, the regional candidate of *Libertad*, had been murdered by a *Sendero Luminoso* commando.

My father was moved. He decided that we must fly to Ayacucho and stand by the widow in her time of grief. A small plane was found and another for the journalists who wanted to go along in case something happened. We didn't inform the authorities because that would have amounted to informing our enemies. In Ayacucho, the atmosphere of tension was evident even in the airport. The walls along the road were covered with the slogans of the *Sendero* and the infamous Rodrigo Franco

Commando. We made our way to the College of Public Accountants, a small flat in an ancient, miserable building, where the members of Julián's humble family were helping his colleagues pack up the dead man's belongings. Women in mourning, their eyes puffy with tears; young men drunk on *chicha de jora*; resigned expressions. In the middle of the room, between the candles, lay Julián Huamaní Yauri in the coffin.

After my father spoke, he and his colleagues carried the coffin through the streets of Ayacucho and, before the eyes of the curious people emerging onto their balconies, we walked until we reached a parish church where we delivered the body.

In the first fifty-five days of the year, violence had taken 600 lives. Two weeks before the elections, José Gálvez Fernández was killed, another martyr of the Alliance. A few days later, as if to demonstrate the arbitrariness of its targets, *Sendero* took the life of Julio Flores—a member of Apra—and planted a bomb a few yards from the Ministry of the Interior. By Friday, 23 March, with the election in full flow, the government declared a state of emergency in Lima and Callao. *Sendero*, in open contempt of the security forces, then ambushed a patrol of seven policemen in a public thoroughfare. All of them died.

My father was always heavily protected. My mother, when she was with him, enjoyed the same protection, and when she wasn't she imagined that she was protected not only by her female bodyguards but by the statistic that few women are attacked in public. My brothers, in danger as long as they stayed in Lima, spent much of their time outside the country finishing their studies. Circumstances seemed to mark me out as the easiest target, with my provocative profile as the Benjamin of Peruvian politics, who had now become the knight of liberal causes and squire of the presidential candidate. Our enemies hated me for being both the son of the candidate and the spokesman for the campaign, and I suspect also because it wasn't my style to hide my thoughts or waste an opportunity to land a punch whenever an enemy dropped his guard. Nor did I see my youth as an obstacle to the fight for freedom, as young men in other times had fought for socialism.

Eighth of April 1990: the Primaries. After voting, we returned to our house in Barranco. All visits were forbidden except for one person: Carmen Balcells, my father's literary agent. Merely by her presence she reminded us that my father had another world that was bigger than politics, which made fewer demands on him, buffeted him less. The atmosphere was calm, and we were able to talk and joke and relax. The threat of Fujimori was well hidden. There was nothing we could do: the die was cast.

At noon we went to the Sheraton Hotel. The presidential suite on the nineteenth floor was reserved for my parents, my brothers, my Uncle Lucho and myself. Orders were strict: nobody could enter without permission, not even Mark Malloch Brown, who had reserved the eighteenth floor for himself and his computers. The moments leading up to the delivery of Mark's first set of projections were tense. The family members and friends waiting outside watched us leaving and entering our room and were convinced that we knew something. Everyone's eyes were fixed on the closed door of the presidential suite. Down below, on the first floor, journalists were struggling to break through the security barriers.

I went down to the eighteenth floor with Lucho at half-past twelve. At a quarter to one Mark showed up; it was impossible for him to conceal his disappointment. We went up together to see my father and tell him the news.

'Things are not going badly,' Mark said. 'At this point you have forty per cent of the vote while Fujimori has about twenty-five per cent. Your vote is tending to increase. The next projection could give you around forty-five per cent. With a result like that you could have a major victory.'

One thing was certain: Fujimori, previously unknown, now existed as a threat, and existed throughout Peru, so much so that Apra had been relegated to third place, while the left had dropped to fourth. But Mark was right: things could be worse; the surveys of the past few days had shown this. Even so, if the vote did not improve, we would have to have a second run-off election. Given the nature of our campaign—that of making changes so profound as to transform the structures of the country—this was a serious set-back.

My father reacted very calmly. 'If the figure stays as it is, the people will have given us the mandate that we need.'

We were to keep quiet and wait for more projections.

At half-past two in the afternoon I entered the private office on the eighteenth floor that had been reserved for television interviews. Jaime Bayly was there, speaking to someone from Channel Four. His pale face and lugubrious voice said it all. The channel's polls gave us thirty-five points and Fujimori wasn't far behind. So much, then, for winning outright at the primaries! But there was also something we hadn't suspected until that moment: the possibility that the laborious run-off elections weren't in the bag either.

Upstairs, on the nineteenth floor, my father was already thinking about what steps to take. 'I can't govern the country like this,' he said to me. 'I'll invite Fujimori publicly to a talk and give him the presidency. Peru has voted for a president in favour of compromise and trickery, one who won't make any changes but will dedicate himself to organizing and administering chaos, and applying sticking-plasters. In no way am I that president.'

'Prepare the press conference,' he then said. 'I'm going down.' Before leaving he had a constitutional consultation with Elias Laroza. He asked him if the candidacy could be abandoned in such conditions, which Laroza interpreted as a question about the legal possibility of Fujimori giving up. 'Yes,' he answered, 'it's perfectly possible.'

Ninth of June 1990: my father closed his campaign with a message to the nation that was highly literary in tone. Peru, he said, is like a book. 'An ancient, beautiful, never-ending book. It contains pages of great beauty telling us of a great civilization built by Peruvians in this very same "roof of the world", pages written on the stones of Machu Picchu and Chavin, in the paintings of Nazca and Paracas, in the gold and silver of the Incas. There are pages of bravery, such as those describing Grau's ship and Bolognesi's sword.' He closed his speech by calling on Peru to write a happy ending.

The following day feelings ran high. We went to vote and

locked ourselves in the house at Barranco. Not the Sheraton, just the peace of the fireside. We had a computer installed in the house that relayed results as they were tabulated at a secret office on the Calle de Kenko. The absentee voters were counted first: we had won more than fifty per cent. Although the national results were not expected for some time, we, as well as the media, had exit-polls to predict the results. By noon Mark Malloch Brown and Freddy Cooper arrived with the first prediction. Something unprecedented had occurred, rendering the last-minute polls conducted the day before pure fantasy. Fujimori was ten points ahead and was solidly defeating us the length and breadth of the country. We were a few points ahead in Lima, but we knew that we needed to be ten or twelve points in front to win the election in the country. But it wasn't so. We didn't even win in Piura, as we had calculated. Mark tried to be reassuring, but my father, after looking carefully at the sheet covered with numbers, concluded that we had lost. There was a short silence. And then he said: 'I feel sorry for Peru.'

At three o'clock in the afternoon, there was a news flash on the television. At five, Fujimori's lead had increased, and by six he was fifteen points ahead. My father, rather than going on television to concede defeat, went to the *Libertad* headquarters, his political cradle, to speak to a furious multitude crying out for the head of the 'Chinaman' and yelling 'Mario for President!' There, in a tense conversation with his party members, surrounded by party operatives unable to hide their tears, he delivered the most beautiful speech of his presidential candidacy.

Translated from the Spanish by Shaun Whiteside

GRANTA

Mark Malloch Brown

The Consultant

When I arrived in Lima in June 1989 to discuss bringing a team of political consultants to advise Mario Vargas Llosa on his campaign, I had an eerie sense of familiarity. Ten years earlier, as a young official of the United Nations, I had overseen the flight into Thailand of the Khmer Rouge and wanted never again to see the sullen look of murderous class and ethnic hatred that I had seen in their eyes. Ten years later, I encountered it in the bus queues in Lima. They were an urban underclass, recent migrants from the countryside who sought to pick a marginal living on the downtown pavements by day and were now waiting for one of the infrequent mini-buses that would carry them to their distant squatter slums. In those glassy brown eyes was a death threat against Peru's old white ruling class. I did not need polling to tell me that Peru was dry tinder.

The leaders of Mario's crusade to renew Peru sat around a table at our first meeting. Several of them had, like him, spent long periods out of the country: all were visibly upper-class. Enrique Ghersi was the darkest-skinned but nobody would have mistaken the well-groomed young lawyer for a representative of the *cholos*, Peru's Indian majority. Mario himself was a man confident among his own people. He was tall, and good-looking, and elegant in a well-cut European sports jacket.

Like Mario I felt that Peru's future was in stabilizing the economy by radical measures—privatizing industry, permitting competition and entrepreneurship. I had seen half-hearted reform programmes fail. Democracy would last in the region only if it could be shown to be consistent with bold leadership. But I also felt that, like marketers of other products, my colleagues and I could make his politics of rapid economic adjustment with its inevitable early consequences of higher real prices and increased unemployment attractive to the consumer. We could do for Mario what Mrs Thatcher's consultants had done for her: to take the hard edge off a radical programme for economic recovery. Our meeting was interrupted by a call (which I had arranged) from the leader of the Bolivian opposition, who had just won an election, with our help, having promised to implement a Thatcher-like economic programme. Goni Sanchez de Lozada had moved from fourth place in the polls to win the popular vote, even though two of the losing parties would eventually form a coalition to keep him out of the presidency. Goni told Mario that the politics of conviction would be enhanced by a scientific campaign; that polling and television could be deployed to strengthen the argument for economic reform. Mario did not have to play the old Latin American populist game of promising a schoolhouse in every village and a new square in every town. He could tell the blunt truth but he must let his advisors 'package' it for him. Mario, anxious for an unequivocal popular vote in favour of his tough free-market reforms, seemed intrigued by our black arts and was determined to make his campaign as modern as he hoped his presidency would be.

Months before, however, Mario had made a dreadful mistake. He had joined his *Libertad* movement with the two major opposition political parties, Popular Action and the Christian Popular Party, in what he thought was a vast national crusade against Alan García and the old left. Instead he became entrapped by the old right. Popular Action and the Christian Popular Party stood for all that was worst in the traditional political order. Backed by the old oligarchy, they had perpetuated an alliance between the state, the unions and a business class that grew rich on the absence of competition. Peruvians held these parties and their leaders responsible, along with García, for the national collapse. Fernando Belaúnde, the aged leader of Popular Action, had preceded García as president. It was his catastrophic last term that had prepared the way for García to take the presidency by a landslide vote. Mario failed to see that the anti-political tide that had initially carried him forward was aimed as much at the dinosaurs of the old right as at his nemesis Alan García, the populist leftist.

Belaúnde and Luis Bedoya, the leader of the Christian Popular Party, had sensed Mario's ambivalence about being a full-time candidate and also suspected he lacked the steel to resist them. They were flexing their muscles and even appeared to be preparing to wrest the presidential nomination from him. Their constant sniping had grown too much for Mario and on the very day of our first meeting he wrote to them renouncing his candidacy and then petulantly set off to receive a literary award in Italy, not realizing that he had inadvertently taken the biggest step towards winning that he could: he had shaken off his allies.

The advice of my colleagues and myself to Mario was: don't mend the pact you have broken. Let the old politicians run against you. It will restore your political independence and make you unbeatable. Mario's concern, which was hard to argue against until we understood the situation more thoroughly, was that he would lose an entire grass-roots organization if he cut his band of *Libertad* intellectuals from the political parties. He did not heed our advice and made peace with the moribund parties.

To most Peruvians it marked a betrayal. The voters were willing to throw aside socialist ideas and even take up the free market crusade, but above all they wanted a break with the old politics. They despised the old politicians and the business class with whom Mario had linked himself. He had bartered away his most precious asset, his independence.

Mario's wife, Patricia, shared our fear of what the politicians would do to Mario's public image and fought to keep him out of their clutches, but her alternative was to build a political base among blonde ladies from upper-middle-class suburbs of Lima. They began as a *Libertad* group that worked in the Lima slums, and it was said against them, by men, that they had persuaded their husbands to contribute the funds to construct the feeding centres, schools and playgrounds they operated. The women, many of whom were impressive and strong-willed, were fighting a battle with their husbands and a male-dominated Peruvian upper class. Their slum work did not help Mario's battle for the barrios. The ladies, often wearing Paris and Milan fashions, were representatives of Vargas Llosa, the rich people's candidate.

When I looked behind the venerable Castilian façade of Peru, I found overtones of white Rhodesia. Many members of the 'old élite' were relatively new settlers who had expected a European lifestyle—built, if necessary, on the backs of the Indians. Throughout the campaign Mario, the son of near-penniless parents, the scholarship boy who charmed

Europe, the internationally renowned writer who was fêted by wealthy Philistines back home, remained a split person. He avoided the social embrace of Peru's white Rhodesians. He was not to be found at their dinner-tables. He abhorred interminable meetings with the politicians. He repeatedly told friends, and his consultants, that the politicians were banal and second-rate—that they had no over-riding ideas to drive their political actions—and constantly sought refuge from them by reading poetry on the small planes that took him to his rallies, saving his mornings as late into the campaign as he could for writing, keeping his evenings for family and close friends, delighting in news about events beyond Peru. Personally he was never sucked into the white Rhodesian milieu. But politically he appeared to have become their spokesman.

Mario allowed himself to be surrounded by white-skinned, blond-haired supporters; he and Patricia seemed flattered by their attentions. Too often the news footage showed him getting in or out of the large armour-plated Volvo he had been lent and entering his expensive-looking home, always accompanied by the undoubtedly necessary bodyguards in dark glasses and blue suits. Latin Americans are familiar with the imagery of cars and guards. Every rich businessman, aware of the kidnapping pandemic, has guards. Mario's guards were seen by Peru's lower classes as the luxury item of a privileged man. And certainly a man in a Volvo was an unlikely leader for the mass of Peruvians who could not afford cars. Mario, who works with words and pages, did not adequately understand the power of electronic visual images.

Mario disregarded the party structures and came to rely on his family, a few friends and his consultants. His inner circle was known as the Royal Family. Patricia was in charge of Mario's schedule; his son, Alvaro, was the press spokesman; Lucho Llosa, Patricia's brother and a producer of low-budget Hollywood movies, oversaw the advertising; Lucho's wife Roxana, a popular (and inevitably blonde) singer, sang the campaign song; even Freddy Cooper, the campaign manager, was a cousin. As families in politics go this was one of the very best. They were smart, open to advice and loyal to each other. In their company I would have some of the most intelligent strategic discussions I have had in any campaign. Decisions would be taken; campaign plans agreed to; ads written and scheduled; Mario's trips planned. Then my colleagues and I would leave, and Mario, who had been the fiercest advocate of strategic campaigning, would be the first to break ranks and go chasing after the day's ephemeral issue: an attack by García, an obscure foreign policy matter. Mario's message got lost in the instant comment or the spontaneous TV spot.

Political communication is two things: definition and repetition. Mario was a master at intellectually defining an issue and a policy. But he avoided repetition. He always moved on to the next item. Mrs Thatcher made dullness a virtue; she never tired of saying the same thing. In Peru, with a simpler electorate grappling with more novel ideas through a less efficient mass media, this aspect of Mrs Thatcher above all others required emulating. It was the one which least interested Vargas Llosa.

In the closing weeks of the first round, Mario insisted on visiting every *departamento* in the country, in an exhausting and dangerous effort to convey his message. He spoke of his childhood dream to be a matador and he conducted a brave campaign. Our poll numbers screamed a warning: return to Lima and campaign in every barrio to stop the rot in the fragile urban vote. But Mario and Patricia were romancing an entire nation as they moved across Peru expounding to huge crowds their dream of privatization and a tight fiscal policy. Before they spoke, local politicians and Mario's blonde-haired sister-in-law, Roxanna, would warm up the audience of townsfolk and *campesinos*. Mario suspended his belief in poll results, and put his faith in the size of his crowds.

Mario had also lost the art of the great platform speech. His delivery was often wooden. A great Latin American stump speech has no counterpart in the cold armchair politics of the Anglo-Saxon world. It is not just a matter of florid Spanish phrases and tub-thumping delivery, but of huge crowds pulsating in front of their leader. Although his first speech in Plaza San Martín, against nationalization, was powerful, Mario's speech-making had become, according to those who were with the campaign from the beginning, impersonal and flat.

I saw his final address in Lima. We had persuaded him to forge a link with the common people by personalizing his presentation and talking about growing up poor in Arequipa. Mario warned us that he could not refashion his speech overnight with well-polished applause lines. The crowd was listless. It was divided between Lima's poor in the plaza and the rich who watched from the windows of the high-rise Sheraton Hotel that overlooked the square. They had taken rooms for the evening. The two Perus did not mix.

By late 1989, it had become clear that Mario was not going to win outright. His vulnerability was evident. He was seen as a man guiltily straining to keep a closet door shut with the bad secret of his allies behind it. He began as a champion of change and ended up being perceived as a protector of privilege. Our research showed that Peruvians sought to distinguish between their respect for Vargas Llosa and their concern about his ability to control those around him.

The campaign against Mario cast him as the class enemy of the poor. One common advertisement was of Peru as a futuristic laboratory being inhumanely experimented on by Mario to a Pink Floyd sound-track. But the greatest threat came from a candidate promising a more modern miracle: change without effort. He was Alberto Fujimori, the son of Japanese immigrant parents, the former rector of the agrarian university and early-morning talk-show host of a television programme on farming.

Fujimori became a dark-skinned Peruvian who had taken on the light-skinned and aristocratic Vargas Llosa. He may have been first-generation Peruvian, but in the war of images he represented the polyglot Peru that had been exploited and marginalized by the European interlopers that Vargas Llosa symbolized. I remember cringing when Vargas Llosa sought to defend his long years of exile by saying he had nothing to be ashamed of because Europe was the future Peru should be striving for. He surrendered to Fujimori's definition of alternative role models for Peru: Japan versus Europe.

When Fujimori's extensive business dealings, as private landlord and absentee landowner, were exposed, it became clear that he was at least as wealthy as Vargas Llosa. Clearly he was less 'Peruvian', in the way Peru's old white class defined it, than Mario. He maintained many Japanese customs. There was debate about whether he had ever been issued a Peruvian passport. Yet to the great mass of voters he was closer to their Peruvian reality than Mario Vargas Llosa, from an old Arequipa family, and from Knightsbridge, London. New theories of mankind's origins began to appear in Peru; shifting land masses and the first migrations had brought the ancestors of Asians and Latin American Indians into contact. Japan's economic success was seen as a reward for hard work and industry that could be enjoyed by small, dark-skinned, non-European races who had broken the European yoke. Japan became a model as well as a potential source of aid and technology.

After the first round, which he narrowly won, Mario was inclined to concede. He could see little purpose in a second round. Friends, politicians, consultants and even the Archbishop (Mario's atheism is well known) persuaded him otherwise. Fujimori was an untested figure and had opportunistically seized Mario's symbols of change without backing them with substance. He might not survive the close scrutiny of a second round; his land deals might arouse controversy. Fujimori himself worried that Mario's withdrawal would deny him legitimacy. Mario considered offering Fujimori a deal—he would give up his candidacy if Fujimori accepted his programme—but then rejected the idea.

The second round was a series of desperate efforts to turn the tide: the Vargas Llosa family drawing the wagons tighter as the politicians and others criticized them for their failure in the first round; renewed attempts to get the ladies and the politicians to organize; our gringo push to launch negative attacks on Fujimori; Mario's reluctance to cheapen the debate in this way.

On election day, while my colleagues and I fussed over the early computer returns, Mario watched the World Cup on television and packed for a trip to Paris to participate in

L'Apostrophe, the French book programme. I suspect that his immediate return to the writer's life was a relief. Yet nobody, least of all someone as self-disciplined as Mario, experiences a futile effort without anger. He had given too much to walk away without being deeply disappointed. In an interview in *El Pais* a week or so later he whimsically speculated that it was all for the best that Peruvians had saved him from the job of president.

There is comfort in having been right. Today President Fujimori is grappling to apply Mario's economic programme of stabilization, with the inevitable economic dislocation and pain that Mario warned of and that Fujimori pretended could be avoided. Charges of betrayal are rife. *Sendero Luminoso* and other terrorist groups have stepped up their violence and the country seems to be sliding towards breakdown. As I write Fujimori is in Japan seeking economic aid and *Sendero* has put out half the country's electricity; it seems unlikely that Mario's longed-for change is at hand. Within months the country's only viable export will probably be cocaine.

Sendero cast a shadow over the election: it intimidated voters, assassinated candidates of Mario's party, but was rarely mentioned in political debate. The presidential palace may be Fujimori's now but Peru's real choices remain what they were before the election: Vargas Llosa's bourgeois reform or *Sendero*'s revolution. The odds favour *Sendero*.

GRANTA

Sergio Larrain
In The Andes

IXAT

GRANTA

SERGIO R[illegible]REZ
ELECTION NIG[illegible] IN
NICARAGUA

It was the best of times, it was the worst of times, it was the age of wisdom, it was the age of foolishness, it was the epoch of belief, it was the epoch of incredulity, it was the season of Light, it was the season of Darkness, it was the spring of hope, it was the winter of despair . . .

The Best of Times

On the night of 17 July 1979, two twin-engined six-seater Cessnas taxied out of the dark hangar at the Juan Santamaria airport in San José, moved on to the runway and lifted into the mist above Costa Rica's central hills. The planes were bound for the city of León in the west of Nicaragua. León had already been liberated by the guerrillas of the Sandinista Front, and I was one of the five members of the Junta of National Reconstruction that would be established there. Travelling with me was Violeta Barrios, the widow of the journalist Pedro Joaquín Chamorro. Daniel Ortega was waiting for us in León.

The plane set its course northwards, and the lights of San José winked through the mist. I tried to make out my own house in the Los Yoses district. My wife, Gertrudis, and I had lived there for the last four years and in the recent months we had learned to co-exist with the crates of medicines and food that filled the living-room, corridors and bedrooms, that Gertrudis would then dispatch to the Sandinista fighters along the southern front who were struggling to take the town of Rivas.

I had said goodbye to Gertrudis and my children an hour earlier, hurriedly stuffing a pair of jeans and a few shirts into a travel bag. All I was leaving them were my books and the Volvo, which had suffered badly from its many trips carrying arms and provisions to the Nicaraguan frontier, but which Gertrudis still drives around the streets of Managua today, more than ten years later.

The plane followed Nicaragua's Pacific coastline. A glorious

Opposite: Sergio Ramirez and Daniel Ortega, at the Sandinista election rally in Managua, 21 February 1990.

Photo: Julio Etchart

moon in what was now a clear night sky illuminated the crests of the waves, which seemed to break motionlessly on the shore. Through the window, I tried to guess from the brightness of the lights which town we were flying over: Rivas, Tola, Nandaime, Jinotepe, Diriamba. Beyond them, deep in the darkness, I could make out the huge halo over Managua. In the early hours, Anastasio Somoza Debayle had fled to Miami with his mistress Dinorah Sampson. His successor, Francisco Urcuoy Maliaño, was stubbornly refusing to relinquish the presidential sash that had been draped across his chest in a comic ceremony held in the Intercontinental Hotel.

When we landed in Nicaragua on a tiny airstrip used by cotton-field crop-dusters and lit by lines of oil lamps, there were only dreams; there was no despair.

The Worst of Times

The next day, 18 July 1979, the Junta of National Reconstruction was installed in León. The ceremony took place in the great hall of the university there. I had graduated as a lawyer in this hall, and my parents had travelled from my home town of Masatepe to see me fulfil their ambition of having a professional among the musicians, small farmers, artisans and shopkeepers of our huge family. In this same hall, Fernando Gordillo and I had started the Ventana literary movement in 1960, reading out an anti-manifesto celebrating the power of revolutionary art. And the year before, in 1959, when I was seventeen and a first-year student, I had walked out of this hall to join a protest in the streets against the attack that the combined forces of Somoza's National Guard and the Honduran army had made on a column of Nicaraguan exiles trying to re-enter the country from Honduras. Soldiers had fired on us, killing four (including two with whom I studied law), and wounding over sixty others. The torn, blood-stained flag we carried at the head of our march was still here in the great hall twenty years later, kept in a glass case beside the platform where I was about to be sworn in as a member of the provisional government.

It seemed a circle was closing: I was returning to my origins as a politician and a writer.

Later that day, we went to Chichigalpa, a village west of León, to attend a meeting in the baseball stadium with the workers from the San Antonio sugar mill. From the improvised platform where I stood, I saw only a dense forest of banners and rifles. Church bells rang out in celebration. It was all confused and dream-like. I was watching a revolution in the warm air of the canefields of the Pacific coast plains.

That night guerrilla columns arrived, appearing out of the hills, following the trails from Tonalá, Somotillo and Villanueva. These were country people, and they had marched in the dark, the noise of their boots and rifles the only sounds as they gradually filled the car park of the Cosigüina Hotel. The hotel was closed to tourists because of the war, but we re-opened it so that the guerrilla fighters could sleep there, guests in a hotel for the first time in their lives. I can still hear my voice urging them, in the darkness, to realize that the land was now theirs.

These were the final moments of a long war, one begun by Sandino in 1927 in his attempt to overthrow the Somoza dictatorship that occupied Nicaragua on behalf of the United States; it was taken up again in 1961 by the Sandinista Front and brought to its conclusion by a general uprising. Thousands and thousands of people had been tortured and murdered.

There was no room in our dreams for another war. The revolution was heralded with the voice of an old testament prophet: restore the poor to their thrones of glory and hand them the sceptres of their power. We were convinced that lasting peace had arrived.

But there was no peace.

The revolution pardoned Somoza's thugs—there were no firing squads, gallows or guillotines—and many had fled to Honduras or Miami where the first Contra terrorist squads were trained by veterans of the Bay of Pigs. And then the gentlemen of the CIA became involved. Counter-revolutionary leaders were put on a payroll, military training camps were set up in Honduras and C-4 explosives appeared magically in the hands of bridge-blowing experts. Our harbours were mined; the fuel storage tanks at Corinto were razed by rockets. No more wheat for Nicaragua: there was suddenly an embargo on trade. No more loans for Nicaragua: there was suddenly a financial blockade. The United States Congress approved arms and ammunition for the counter-revolution; Nicaragua was to beg for mercy if it wanted to be absolved of its sins. Then: covert aid, Oliver North, fields ravaged, harvests destroyed, peasant co-operatives burned to the ground, rural schools and health clinics under fire from mortars Made in the USA. There were so many coffins that there were not enough nails.

I mention this not in a spirit of bitterness, but because this era is already being consigned to the past. The word Contra, so familiar from its constant appearance in the pages of newspapers, will gradually be forgotten except for the occasional mention in 'Rambo' style films. 'I am a Contra too,' was the slogan President Reagan showed on his T-shirt—for television.

The Age of Wisdom

On 22 December 1974, a guerrilla commando group attacked the residence of José Maria Castillo, one of Somoza's closest associates, while he was holding a reception in honour of the United States Ambassador, Turner B. Shelton. Shelton had left a short while earlier, but the other guests, including Somoza's relatives, ministers, businessmen, ambassadors and their wives, were taken hostage.

Somoza was compelled to accede to the guerrillas' demands, releasing all the Sandinistas held in his jails (Daniel Ortega among them), paying a ransom of a million dollars and allowing a Sandinista Front proclamation to be read on national television and radio. Suddenly, the whole world knew that the Sandinista Front existed.

About six months later I arrived in Costa Rica after completing a novel that I had written while abroad. At the end of that year, Daniel Ortega's brother Humberto arrived secretly, and from then on we worked together to create the political organization of the Sandinista Front, allying with the others opposed to Somoza and building a mass movement which would draw from every social class of the population, with, we hoped, the support of Latin American and European governments and political parties. We wanted a government of national unity, one in which the business sector would also play an important part.

In March 1977 I discussed these ideas with Daniel Ortega. He was in San José preparing for the insurrection that would start in October. Our political programme—revolutionary for a revolutionary party—was more specifically defined at this meeting: a mixed economy, political pluralism, international non-alignment. Daniel called on me to organize secretly a provisional government, and over the following months we enlisted the support of twelve prominent Nicaraguans—among them, a Maryknoll priest (Miguel de Escoto), a Jesuit priest (Fernando Cardenal), the owner of a chain of supermarkets (Felipe Mántica), the owner of a factory making instant coffee (Emilio Baltodano), a lawyer (Joaquín Cuadra Chamorro), an economist who worked for the Inter-American Development Bank in Washington (Arturo Cruz), and a former rector of the national university (Doctor Carlos Tünnermann). I was made head of the group.

The October offensive failed. It began, however, a new phase in Nicaragua's history. Somoza suffered a heart attack. The open raids on military barracks, including one outside Managua, proved that the National Guard was vulnerable, and further attacks could now follow. It was also then that our provisional government emerged: the Group of Twelve, as we were known, which issued a communiqué from Costa Rica, giving our full support to the Sandinista Front.

In January 1978, three months after the insurrection, the people of Managua burned the businesses owned by Somoza in protest at the killing of the journalist Pedro Joaquín Chamorro by a gang of thugs hired by Somoza's son. The next month the people of Monimbó rose in revolt, their ancestral drums beating, fighting tanks with home-made bombs and hunting rifles, their faces hidden behind masks usually worn for traditional dances.

And by August, the Group of Twelve was able to return to Nicaragua, defying warrants for our arrest. Over 200,000 people filled the streets of Managua to welcome us, and huge demonstrations greeted us as we toured the country. That same month a guerrilla commando group disguised as members of the EEBI, the crack troops of Somoza's National Guard, stormed the national palace in Managua while the members of parliament were in session. They were taken hostage, and Somoza once more found himself forced to negotiate and agree to the release of prisoners.

We, meanwhile, were forced back into hiding.

There was another offensive in September, and the fighting spread to Managua, León, Matagalpa, Esteli, Masaya, Diriamba, Chinandega—the most important towns of Nicaragua. The dictator was losing his hold on power, while the United States' attempts to preserve the National Guard, even without Somoza, were becoming increasingly desperate. The Group of Twelve re-emerged from hiding—it was time to represent the Sandinista Front in the subsequent negotiations—and we succeeded in blocking all the moves by the United States to install a Somoza regime without Somoza.

Then: 19 July 1979, and the triumph of the final insurrection. Somoza was gone; the dictatorship was gone and the National Guard with it. We set up the same broad-based government of national unity that we had planned in 1977. The way seemed clear to achieve true independence for Nicaragua.

The Age of Foolishness

In October 1984 I went by helicopter to San Carlos, a tiny port near the Costa Rican border where Lake Nicaragua meets the San Juan river. It was the anniversary of our first insurrection. From the helicopter, I could see the isthmus of Rivas, a narrow strip of land bounded by the Pacific Ocean on one side, and the cattle-rearing plains on the other. Behind me, rising from the slate-coloured waters of the lake, were the twin volcanoes of El

Concepción and El Maderas, their summits shrouded as ever in cloud. It is a landscape that has always astonished me. I had come here last on a secret visit in 1976 with the Argentine writer Julio Cortázar, who had shared my wonder at the beauty of the region.

The peasant farmers and fishermen of San Carlos had gathered in the local baseball stadium. From where I stood, I could see the still water of the lake, the hills, the river disappearing into the jungle and, in the far distance, the blue mountains of Costa Rica. The men wore straw hats and rubber boots, and many of the women had children at their breasts. Red and black Sandinista flags extended in the warm breeze that carried the smells of salt fish and cow dung.

During the ceremony a peasant from Morrito was to hand over his rifle to me in public. He had been fighting for the counter-revolution but had laid down his arms a few days earlier. A gaunt, little man in poor clothes climbed on to the platform, looking just like a plucked bird. He was holding an FAL rifle which had a piece of rope for a strap.

The dreams of our revolution.

This little man, cowed by the spectacle, dropped his rifle into my hands and vanished. What world existed inside his head? I found myself asking. Was my world different? Were the two worlds connected? Had a connection ever existed?

I thought I had a clear picture of our confrontation with the United States: a nation against an empire, a new society fighting against those who sought to preserve the old order. I wrote and talked repeatedly about the conflict. I was committed to providing that peasant and his family with a new way of life. I wanted to give him back the land which had been stolen from his ancestors and modern tools with which to work it. I wanted him to have new seeds, and agricultural machinery, and a guaranteed price for his crops.

But, attempting to re-organize his life from our far-off centres of revolutionary power, we were imposing our ideas of freedom on him. To prevent the land falling back into the greediest hands, as it had done in the past, we made land titles non-transferable. It took us a long time to accept that the peasants wanted no strings to their land ownership deeds. We were losing the peasants, and our plans for collectivized farming seriously undermined all possibility of winning them over to our project.

And, of course, the world of the little, bird-like man—bound by the four palm-tree walls of his hut and the hills around him—was being torn apart in the war. All the time, there were whispers: the Sandinistas don't believe in your religion! They'll separate you from your children and force you to work in a co-operative! They'll tell you the price of your crops! They'll make you fight in their war! In the end his fears had proved stronger than our promises. That was why the counter-revolutionary war gradually became a peasant war, dividing the peasants into those who understood the revolution, and those who could not be reached by it. Soon, the ancient rifles like the one I was handed by the peasant at Morrito were being replaced by thousands of new ones, from the United States arsenals, dropped from planes paid for by the CIA, and with them ground-to-air missiles, grenade launchers, sophisticated radio equipment, boots, uniforms, field rations.

Hundreds of millions of dollars were spent to destroy our passionate, stubborn dream of the future. Not to destroy our mistakes—we were trying to correct them ourselves—but to erase the example of a small country which had the nerve to stand on its own for the first time in its history.

The Epoch of Belief

From 20 July 1979, we were able to move cautiously around Managua but were constantly being stopped and asked to identify ourselves. Although we were the leaders of a government, our faces were almost unknown: we had never appeared in newspapers or on television. We found a polaroid camera in an abandoned government office and clipped a card with our photo and name to our shirt pockets.

The guerrilla troops set up their headquarters in Somoza's bunker and the new government moved next to the bunker, into the old Intercontinental Hotel. Daniel Ortega and I stayed in adjacent rooms. Decisions were made in the café or in the corridors. We were constantly pursued by a swarm of people: relatives of soldiers in Somoza's army who had been taken prisoner; mothers of guerrilla fighters looking for their lost sons and daughters; mayors from remote villages who had rushed to seek instructions from us the minute they had been elected; new ambassadors in formal dress trying to present their credentials; cattle ranchers waving IOUs, who had come for payment of meat supplied to the guerrillas; foreign investors who appeared from nowhere to talk of fantastic opportunities; people with schemes to recover Somoza's fortune from Swiss banks; peasants with bottles full of oily water from places where they claimed petrol was oozing out of the ground, or with samples of iridescent rocks they said promised a fortune in precious minerals.

A few days later we discovered some empty offices in the Central Bank, one of two skyscrapers in the heart of the city centre not destroyed by the 1972 earthquake. Only four floors of its original seventeen had survived, and it was there that we installed the government. It was as if everything had been miraculously awaiting us: desks, filing-cabinets, telephones, typewriters, a porcelain coffee service inscribed with the Central Bank insignia. The government was located on the fourth floor. We all had large windows overlooking the ruins of the city; the only room which also had decorative plants and leather armchairs was allocated to Dona Violeta de Chamorro.

We set to work at a huge table; a table large enough to accommodate the floods of people who wanted to see us. Our work sessions lasted until dawn. In those first days of creation, when everything was without form, we made and unmade the world with decrees read out on national radio.

The Epoch of Incredulity

In the summer of 1980, over 60,000 secondary schoolchildren and university students went out into the country to teach people to read and write.

Over sixty per cent of the population was illiterate—in the isolated mountain areas the illiteracy was complete—and lorries and buses left at dawn transporting the young teachers, some still children, carrying their weapons in their backpacks: pencils, exercise books and primers. The teachers were organized in fronts, like guerrilla formations, one for each region. The National Literacy Crusade was a second insurrection.

My two eldest children joined the crusade. My son Sergio was sent to Muan, on the Atlantic coast, and Maria, my daughter, went to the village of Los Garcia. At weekends, my wife and I visited them with food and sweets and encouragement—as many thousands of other parents did, overcoming the obstacles of rural travel to be with their children in the remotest regions.

The young teachers lived with the peasant families—the girls helping with the housework, cooking and milking the cows, while the boys worked in the fields. Then in the afternoons in the simple rural schools or under village trees, and in the evenings by the light of lamps they had brought with them, the young teachers gathered the people to teach them the alphabet and to show them on a blackboard the meaning of words they were hearing for the first time. For six months Nicaragua became one huge school.

I received letters from people writing for the first time. But it was during this period that the violent past claimed its first victim. Somoza's National Guard, regrouped in Honduras, crossed the border and killed a peasant teacher, Georgino Andrade. He was killed because he was teaching people to read. Somoza's supporters said our teaching was totalitarian, that the literacy crusade was brainwashing. Later they would kill the leaders of rural co-operatives, health brigade workers, young people constructing roads through the mountains, experts in animal husbandry or artificial insemination.

By the end of the campaign, though, illiteracy in Nicaragua had been reduced to around twelve per cent of the population. We celebrated the success in the Plaza 19 de Julio in Managua before a huge crowd of young people. Each village in Nicaragua now has a school. There is no reason for the dream to end.

The Season of Light

The Avenida Roosevelt, where we established our government in 1979, was named by General Anastasio Somoza, the first Somoza, after an official visit he made to Washington in 1944. He was received with full honours by the president. A guard of West Point cadets lined Pennsylvania Avenue; there was a fly-past and a gun salute. When someone asked Roosevelt why there was such a display for the dictator of a banana republic, he replied with his famous phrase: 'He's a son of a bitch, but he's our son of a bitch.' Somoza either did not know, or made sure not to let on, that the lavish reception was actually a rehearsal for the visit of George VI of Britain, who arrived a few days later.

Nearly all the buildings along the Avenida Roosevelt were damaged or destroyed in the 1972 earthquake. One that survived was the National Bank where the first Somoza's men, carrying bags of money under one arm and Thompson sub-machine guns under the other, would appear at the sales auctioning repossessed estates—cattle ranches, coffee plantations—and buy them up for next-to-nothing. No one else dared offer a better price. The new national assembly now sits in that building. The representatives of the coalition which backs Violeta de Chamorro sits to the right of the floor; we Sandinistas are on the left. Since the transfer of power, there have not been many sessions, but there have been enough for us to see that the right is using its majority to abolish, without much discussion, the main features of our labour laws.

A motion is before the assembly to return properties to Somoza supporters which the revolution had confiscated. The intention is obviously to dismantle the popular gains made by the Sandinista revolution and to restore all the former privileges.

To the right of the Sandinistas sit fifty-one deputies. The Sandinista deputies number thirty-nine. These people have bullet scars on their chests and arms, or the marks of torture to testify to long years spent in jail. They are the ones who lit the dark night of the Somoza era with fire. They now sit on the opposition benches of the democratic national assembly, made possible by the revolution—guerrillas who, for the first time in the whole history of armed revolution, have accepted their roles as members of the opposition out of respect for a popular vote.

The Season of Darkness

Pedrarias Davíla, the first Spanish governor in Nicaragua, introduced a reign of darkness that lasted for centuries. He took possession of all the arable lands of the Pacific coast, all the cattle, the gold mines and all the native Indians. He had his enemies' heads chopped off in the main square of León, which he made the capital of his empire. He also had prayers for the dead sung over him while he lay, alive, on the cathedral's high altar.

Davíla was nearly ninety when he died, leaving all his power and possessions to his grandsons, the Contreras brothers. The pair of them died while trying to extend slavery south to Panama and Peru. They were Nicaragua's first dynasty, the first Somozas.

Seasons of darkness followed: in 1910, United States marines came to protect the canal route through Nicaragua and handed the country over to the bankers of the Morgan Trust Company. Our oligarchy welcomed the marine generals and colonels; its bishops blessed the invaders' weapons. General Benjamin Zeledón, who resisted the invasion in Coyotepe Fort, was hunted by the marines and killed in an ambush. His body was dragged by a pair of oxen through the streets of Catarína (an incident witnessed by Sandino as a boy and never forgotten).

The first Somoza grew richer and richer under the protection of the United States, robbing and murdering until he became the owner of all the arable land, all the cattle, all the gold mines, just as Pedrarias Davíla had. Sandino's Army of the Defence of National Sovereignty held off the marines for six years in the Las Segovias mountains with ancient rifles and bombs made from sardine tins left in the invaders' camps. In 1934 Sandino was murdered on the orders of Somoza, and his army was pursued through the mountains until it was wiped out by the National Guard. Then, the kingdom of darkness once more: the blackness of the prisons and the torture chambers and the cages in Somoza's private zoo where political prisoners were kept.

I was thinking of this recently when the new mayor of Managua celebrated taking office in the gardens of the Intercontinental Hotel. He had also been a judge under Somoza, and had sentenced many Sandinistas to his jails. The fiesta was like those of times gone by. Among those present were Silvio Argüello Cardenal, owner of cotton plantations, a vice-president during one of Somoza's terms as president; Adolfo Calero, leader of the counter-revolutionaries; the Cuban mayor of Miami; and Lieutenant Hislop, a torturer in Somoza's security police. Also present were those who had returned from Miami to reclaim properties confiscated in the revolution. They made a great show of hugging and embracing each other. The same gallows faces under the television lights; the same suits and ties; the same solid gold watches; the same diamond rings. They all wore dark glasses although it was night.

The Spring of Hope

In the first days after the revolution, we went round baptizing everything with the names of fallen comrades. One of our first laws prohibited the names of living people from being given to public places, or their photographs or portraits from being publicly displayed, or their birthdays from being celebrated. It was different under Somoza: Puerto Somoza, Villa Somoza, Estadio Somoza, Colonia Somoza; the day of the army was the birthday of the first Somoza's wife. The last Somoza demanded to be serenaded on each birthday—a mariachi band played—and public employees were forced to gather outside his residence at midnight to wait to see if the dictator would deign to come out to thank them for their congratulations. They had also to pay for gifts out of their wretched salaries (it was hard to find gifts for Somoza, the man who had everything).

After losing last year's elections, we realized that no Sandinista militants, whether minister of state or grass-roots activist, had any possessions—not even the house they were living in. Many had given all they had inherited to the state; others had done their best on poor pay. We then passed a law granting the title deeds of all state-owned properties to the families living in them. Depending on their size, the houses were either given free or sold on mortgages. We adopted this measure after long debate, but it was immediately seized on by the right: we, who owned nothing, suddenly found ourselves accused of plundering the state.

I remember a guerrilla fighter telling me that his most difficult test had been passing the house where he was born, where his parents lay asleep, and not stopping. During these past ten years there have been many nights when I have returned home late and my house was in darkness and I realized that I was neglecting my home. All the hours I have spent away from my wife and children cannot be recovered. My mother in Masatepe used to try constantly to get me on the telephone to ask when I would be visiting.

It was worth not writing the books I shall never now have time to write. It was worth sacrificing my writing career. Others have sacrificed much more: they lost their lives high in the mountains, or, like Julio Buitrago, died fighting alone against entire battalions, or, like the poet Leonel Rugama, refused to surrender while they could still breathe.

Many more sleepless hours await us if the Sandinista Front is to govern Nicaragua again. My house in darkness at midnight; my books for ever about to be written.

The Winter of Despair

Early on the evening of 25 February 1990, I returned home for a shower, wanting to get back to the campaign headquarters by nine. That was when the first election results would start to come in. By ten o'clock, we hoped to have a reliable forecast from the computers.

I had voted with my wife and the children in our own neighbourhood a few blocks from my house. Cameramen and journalists were waiting as we came out after casting our votes—there were more than 1,500 of them in Nicaragua that day—and I told them confidently that the people of Nicaragua were voting for peace, for the end of a war that had been going on for eight long years. Daniel Ortega had voted in his own district of Altagracia, and we had spoken on the telephone shortly before I left home. Reports indicated that there was no trouble and that great numbers of people were waiting in orderly lines to vote. There were international observers at every polling booth.

We had wanted these elections to be the most closely scrutinized in the history of Nicaragua. We had also brought them forward—according to the constitution they were due in November—since we knew that the war could only end once we had elections that were declared to be free and fair by hundreds of independent observers. We saw this as the only way to force the United States to end its support of the armed counter-revolution, to lift its trade blockade and its financial boycott; to accept that the will of the Nicaraguan people be respected; to let us get on with the rebuilding of our country.

The electoral laws were revised to satisfy every possible demand: we even changed the ink that was used for fingerprinting the voters. We accepted that Violeta Chamorro's opposition coalition would be financed with money from the United States.

For ten years foreigners had put us under a huge microscope, examining everything we did. But we had learned to reply patiently to all those who wanted to question us, however arrogant their manner.

I had devoted the previous day to receiving the observers in the Olof Palme Conference Centre. I remember one, a member of the Chilean Electoral Council, asking: 'How do you feel about so many foreigners poking their noses in like this? I feel very bad about it. I feel we are abusing your hospitality. You are the representative of a sovereign government, and I feel ashamed to be here, meddling in the internal affairs of Nicaragua.'

I told him that if we wanted a lasting peace for Nicaragua, I was obliged to keep my deepest feelings to myself.

We had no plan for the eventuality of losing. I was completely confident of victory when I spoke to the foreign observers and to the members of the international press. This was not because like any candidate I refused to contemplate defeat, but because I believed that the revolution had taken deep enough root not to be overturned in any elections. Once again we were pitting our nation against an empire, and despite all the difficulties brought on by the war—the restrictions, the shortages, the general insecurity and fear—the voters would never turn their backs on the Sandinistas. I was convinced of this both emotionally and intellectually; the opinion polls, carried out carefully every fortnight, agreed with the ones done by the foreign companies: they showed a clear victory for us. Our closing rally, in Managua on 21 February, was attended by 500,000 people.

We realized later that many in the crowd had come to hear what we had to offer to end the war, conscription and the economic crisis. They wanted to know what kind of relationship they could expect with the United States. If the Sandinista government were re-elected, would the United States end its aggression? Would it stop supplying the Contras? Would it lift the economic blockade? We failed to answer those questions. We could not reply, because the answer did not depend on us.

In Washington, President Bush declared: if the Sandinistas remain in power, the Contras will go on; the war will go on; the blockade will go on.

We did not realize how deeply this threat affected people who had undergone so many years of suffering. Many suffered again as they voted against us.

Our mistakes didn't help. We had changed direction; we had used methods that were out-of-date; in the areas of the country suffering from the war, we had improvised and been arrogant and had lost sight of important elements of political reality. Despite the opinion polls, we, members of a party with deep popular roots, should have known the hidden feelings of thousands of voters who did not believe there was any chance of the Sandinista Front being able to offer them peace. Could we have persuaded them to change their minds?

When I returned to our campaign headquarters on 25 February, I left my wife behind at the house, preparing for a celebration to which the neighbours had been invited. I agreed to phone her once the first results came in and promised to drop in to the party for a while at least, although I was doubtful that I would be able to keep my promise. Thousands of our supporters were already gathering under the floodlights of the Plaza 19 de Julio next to our headquarters. Daniel and I were supposed to make an appearance there in a few hours.

Shortly after nine o'clock, the first calculations for our sample began to arrive. They were from twelve electoral districts in Masaya: we were losing in eight, winning in four. A few minutes later, we had news of another twelve districts in Managua: we were losing in all twelve. In León, where the Sandinistas had always been strong, we were losing in seven, and ahead in the other eight.

Looking up, I saw Bayardo Arce, our campaign manager, staring anxiously at me. The telephones were ringing constantly, people rushed in and out with messages.

'I don't like the look of this,' Bayardo Arce said.

I suggested we take a smaller sample without waiting for ten per cent of the votes to be counted. We called over Paul Oquist, who was in charge of the computers, and he agreed to make a sample from four per cent of the votes chosen at random, which would be ready in half an hour.

Daniel Ortega rang me to ask how things were going.

'You'd better come over,' I said.

'You sound worried, doctor,' he laughed.

'Just come over.'

He arrived ten minutes later. Our fears had grown, and we told him so. Things did not look good—although of course, there was always a margin of error, and it was too soon to predict for sure. The mind always creates possibilities to protect itself from what it does not want to know.

Soon afterwards we were called into the computer room next

door. The random four per cent sample taken from all nine electoral regions throughout the country gave fifty-four per cent to Violeta Chamorro's party, the UNO, and forty-two per cent to the Sandinista Front. I asked Paul Oquist if the tendency was irreversible.

He replied without hesitation, straining to keep his voice calm and firm. 'It is irreversible.'

'Well then,' I said, turning to Daniel and Bayardo, 'we've lost.'

Outside in the square, the first firecrackers celebrating our expected victory were going off; music was playing through the loud-speakers; people were singing. The fiesta was about to begin.

Before midnight an emergency session of the Sandinista leadership agreed that the election results must be respected. It was a unanimous decision. We asked to meet the heads of the teams of observers: Joao Clemente Baena Soares, general secretary of the Organization of American States; Elliot Richardson, who represented the United Nations; and ex-president Jimmy Carter.

Daniel, Bayardo and I met them in our campaign headquarters at one in the morning. We asked them to inform Violeta Chamorro that if the tendency of the results so far was confirmed, as soon as fifty per cent of the votes had been counted Daniel was prepared to address the nation on radio and television. We also asked them to tell her that the Sandinista Front was prepared to begin an orderly transfer of government.

It was three in the morning when I returned home. This time the lights were still on, and my house was full of anxious, incredulous friends and neighbours who were about to set off for the Plaza 19 de Julio after hearing on the television that we had been defeated. My wife wanted them all to go to the main square to be with our supporters, but our supporters had already slipped away in utter confusion. The floodlights had been turned out; the music was no longer playing over the loud-speakers.

I tried to explain what had happened. I told them Daniel would be speaking first thing in the morning. Then I went to my bedroom while they all silently went their own ways. In the dark,

I embraced my wife.

I did not cry when Eduardo Contreras, Camilo Ortega, Israel Lewites and countless other *compañeros* had been killed. I had choked back my tears of despair and rage. Nor did I cry at the deaths of my father or my elder sister Luisa; even though grief had overcome me like a wave, my jaw had remained firmly clenched. But that dawn for the first time in my life the tears I had always denied burst their banks. It was the saddest moment I have ever known.

At six that morning I was due to meet Daniel in the Olof Palme centre to accompany him when he appeared in public. As I left home, I met Father Ernesto Cardenal, a close neighbour. An early riser, he had gone to bed the previous evening certain that we would win the elections. He could not believe what I told him. I had to assure him that it was true: it was all lost; there was nothing we could do. He sat down hard on the kerb, and when I left him he was still sitting there, with his head in his hands,

When Daniel and I entered the main conference hall, the hundreds of mainly foreign journalists who were waiting for us stood up and gave us a lengthy, emotional ovation. Many of them wept openly. A lot of them had been critics of the revolution and had searched out our faults and judged us mercilessly, but now they were witnessing an immense injustice committed against a besieged nation which had been forced to choose when on the verge of despair. That at least is how I understood their tears.

The dawn announced itself in soft pink and orange tones through the windows of the conference centre. Daniel referred to that dawn as he spoke into the battery of microphones. He spoke calmly and firmly. He was composed, lucid and measured like a true statesman. He gave one of the best speeches of his life. He recalled prison and death, the sacrifices, the spirit of all those who had made the victory of the revolution possible, the courage shown by thousands of Nicaraguans in defence of their country against foreign aggression all through the glorious years of the decade. He reminded everyone that we had no intention of clinging to power, and that we were leaving office as poor as when we had arrived.

I went back home again to try to get some sleep. The streets were absolutely silent. There wasn't a single firecracker to celebrate victory over the Sandinista Front; not one car horn was being hooted. A day of mourning was beginning; the warm wind tugged at our red-and-black election campaign flags hanging on the unlit lamp-posts.

When I stopped at a red light on the corner of the Pista de la Resistencia, a red-eyed newspaper vendor came over. She banged on my car window, and when I lowered it, she grasped my arm.

'Don't hand over the weapons!' she urged me.

But I was done with tears. True revolutions never die. The month of May wasn't far off. The rains would soon be here to revive the parched land and turn the trees and plants green again.

Translated from the Spanish by Nick Caistor

GRANTA

George Steiner
Proofs

Proofs

For Jeanne and Daniel Singer

Now the burn seemed to smart behind his eyes.

Thirty years and more a master of his craft. The quickest, most accurate of proof-readers and correctors in the whole city, perhaps in the province. Working every night, and through the night. So that the legal records, deeds of sale, notifications of public finance, contracts, quotations on the bourse, would appear in the morning, flawless, exact to the decimal point. He had no rival in the arts of scruple. They gave him the smallest print to check, the longest columns of figures to justify, the interminable catalogues of lost and found objects to be auctioned for the post office and public transport. His proof-readings of the biannual telephone directory, of electoral and census rolls, of municipal minutes, were legend. Printing works, the public record office, the courts of law vied for his labours.

But now the sensation of burning, just behind his eyes, felt sharper.

A lifetime inhaling the tang of fresh ink, of lead warm to the touch. The linoleum in his cubicle, his sanctum of the unerring, shook to the beat of the presses. Rotogravure, linotype, electronic type-casting, photo-engraving—he had seen them all. He had outwitted the imperfections, the recursive bugs, the clotted snarls and gremlin upsets of each technique. He knew the provenance, weight, watermark, fibre content, resistance to ink-roller and hot metal of diverse papers by the antennae in his thumb. As he knew the impatient awe of the sub-editor, stock-market messenger, auctioneer, bank clerk, notary public poised at the door of his cell, waiting for the discrete, singular check-mark, his as famous as the colophon of a renowned designer or the signature of a great artist. The incision of his pencil or ball-point at the extreme right-hand bottom corner of the page signifying: *nihil obstat*, this text is ready, error-free, sanctified by precision. Let it be printed, published, franked, mailed to reader

Opposite: L'unitá Festival, 1952, Turin.

Photo: Communist Party Archive

or taxpayer, to client or dealer, to litigant or advocate. There to order and dishevel the world as only print can. Codex, pandect, register, the pamphlet or the tome. Now check-marked. His mark, sometimes before the ink was entirely dry. Legendary as is all perfection.

And with the burn, like a thread of smoke, a blur.

He who had never known the weariness of other proof-readers. Their migraines. Their losses of concentration and trembling fingers. The law students and unemployed lawyers who read proofs for libel in the late evening or early morning stared at him blear-eyed and envious. The firm in charge of printing lists of shareholders for market flotations had, in irked humour, offered a prize for anyone who could spot an error, be it a false initial, in his work. The bottle of champagne remained uncollected. He had heard a tale of proof-readers in another country, men no more schooled than he was, who had corrected the formal arguments in an august work of mathematical logic simply because they observed irregularities in the prescribed system of symbolic and algebraic notations. The story filled him with pride. Once an antique dealer, waiting for his catalogue of manuscripts, autographs and curiosa to be proof-read, had recounted a strange story of a printing error that transmuted the lines of a paltry Elizabethan poet into inviolate gold. Some vagabond had written banalities of a lady whose hair was greying, from whose hair a former brightness had fallen—of which cliché a hurried printer had made the words 'a brightness falls from the air.' To those for whom the language lives, the poetaster was now immortal. He both cherished and hated that anecdote. It made him feel strangely ill like the smell of sex in his younger years. Any *erratum* is a final untruth.

He rubbed his eyes. The forbidden, hitherto unnecessary gesture. The savour of ink and cigarette ash on the back of his hands was, momentarily, pungent. Behind and below him the presses were hammering.

It was the instant he loved best, almost childishly. At the ebb of night when he restored the finely-sharpened pencils to their case, the frayed one in which his father had kept his straight-edged razors, and replaced the congeries of erasers, corrector-fluids and masking-tape in the right-hand drawer, and switched off the light. After which he locked the door to his cubicle and touched his cap, in discrete valediction, to the printers, messengers and packers on the loud floor below. Next he emerged through the small heavy door into first light. Into the first breath of the coming day. The thermos under his arm was now empty. Also the sandwich bag, unless the cadence of the night's deadlines had been too pressing. If empty, he dropped it into the bin at the corner. He hated litter. Waste paper struck him as the very waste of waste. A devastation. At times, if the winds blew a piece towards his feet, he would pick it up, smooth it, read closely and make any correction needed. Then he would deposit it in the garbage receptacle, feeling obscurely rewarded and saddened. Any witness to this rite would have thought him deranged. But he did not cut a conspicuous figure.

He stood, waiting for morning to print shadows on the warehouse roof. There paper was stacked in leviathan rolls, waiting for the delivery trucks and messengers' mopeds to bark into life. He felt the cool of dawn on his skin. The sheer mad wonder of sunrise, even when it was veiled or rain-swept. Even when it was little more than a lost sheen behind the frequent fogs. He turned slightly eastward, towards the native place of morning. Then down the metal steps, towards the square and the tram which would take him home.

2

He was thoroughly familiar to the tram-drivers and ticket-inspectors on their milk-run. Among themselves they called him Owl. Not only because of his night-job and the ruffled, blinking mien with which he mounted the streetcar platform, but for the way in which, his frayed pea-green muffler wound around his thin neck, he perched immediately behind the conductor, closely observant. Exact craft fascinated and consoled him. He took renewed pleasure each morning in the driver's measured touch of the starting-lever, in the flick he gave the brake-handle, in the fine gauging which seemed to guide the exact speed at which he took the tight clanging curve that led into Via Grande. In the late afternoon or early evening, in turn, when journeying back to work, he savoured the adjustments conductors made to balance their cars when they were thronged, when more and more passengers, homeward bound, elbowed their way through the automatic doors. Eyes shut, he could, according to the lurch of the tram and the particular sound of the grinding gears and overhead wires, tell unerringly where he was, and at which of the eleven stops between Santa Lucia and the printing works the car was whining to a halt. Sometimes he and the inspector exchanged views. But he was not spendthrift of words. There had been too many through the night; there would be too many more during the night ahead, minuscule, tightly aligned, prodigal of mistakes.

Why converse when he could scan the city as it passed? He knew his transit by heart. Façade by façade, street-corner by street-corner, each junction inwardly mapped. He knew the cobble-stones which led down an alley from Piazza Borromeo to the glass-blowing manufacture in which his father had had his lungs shredded by searing dust (compensation had been refused). As the tram rattled on, he could peruse the house-fronts, the names over the shops. At the merest glance. The texts changed. Buildings were torn down and remade. He had seen small archipelagos of green tarred over and flower-beds uprooted. A garage now stood where there had been the malodorous, choked Fountain of the Three Masks. To be noted most alertly was the coming and going of placards, billboards, national, regional and civic notices, graffiti, which his eyes had taken in untiringly as the tram slowed or accelerated.

The memory of the marmoreal and Augustan placards of triumph, that man on his white horse, his chins mountainous, remained heavy inside him. He could visualize still the letters in flame-red on the call-up notices, on the decrees of rejoicing or retribution. Unforgettable were the ochre and black—the brazen type-face of the roll of hostages executed in vengeance. After the liberation came the plethora of election posters with their sheaves of grain, Phrygian caps, roosters crowing to azure skies, hammers and sickles, and laurelled women with bounding children at their heels. A flaking, perpetually changing palimpsest which he had to leaf through at speed as the tram churned by. With the raucous years, posters had been glued on posters, promise on promise, edicts of fiscal reform preceding edicts, each in turn scissored by the winds that came from the nearby mountains in the blue of late September, then discoloured and made soggy refuse by the winter rains.

Now the placards and inscriptions were different. They proclaimed lagoons, platinum beaches, palmy cruises on the never-never. Overnight deities of pop beckoned. Hamburgers house-high, softly ebullient with the blood-tide of ketchup. There flashed past the leather twist of the horror film. Everywhere bodies shone bronze yet ethereal. A world so neon-lit, so thrustingly on offer that it demanded to be viewed through those sun-glasses, harlequinned and dolphin-tailed. The fonts, the leading, the designs sickened him. Brutal machine-work. He seemed to hear the pulping of silent forests being pounded to dust so as to produce the lettering used on lavatory tiles. Nevertheless, he could not turn away. On each tram journey he read on, mesmerized.

As he neared home, the shops were opening. His needs were few and pedantically habitual. He drank his coffee under the arcades on Liberation Square. Then bought his bread in one of the very few small bakeries left in the district. He had weaknesses: for sardines lightly grilled, for anchovies from the Balearic Islands (the western Mediterranean having become, as headlines proclaimed, a 'cesspit'). He chose his cheeses with deliberation. The narrow, cavernous shop stayed cool even in the weeks of white heat. He favoured goat-cheese and, especially, a gritty variety from the interior of Sardinia. On occasion, he lingered over the fruit and vegetable stalls. They had been grey and fibrous at the end of the war and for some time after. Now they beckoned, chromatic and opulent as a Persian carpet. Offering plump asparagus, pink grapefruit, blood-oranges, egg-plant, broccoli in profusion. He palped the peppers gently, letting his thumb luxuriate in their clefts. He bought eggs, ground coffee, two bars of soap (there was a sale on), washing-powder, and proceeded up the stairs to his two-room apartment, now called 'studio' even in this undistinguished quarter.

Having put the shopping-bag at his feet he unlocked the double lock. Break-ins were everyday. He had gone up the four flights breathing easily. Having put away his purchases and slipped out of his scarf and jacket, he tested. He opened the window and looked steadily in the direction of the dome of the basilica of the Blessed Martyrs. It rose westward, in a direct line across the morning-lit sea of roofs. Testing. He knew that the dolphin rampant on the ancient weather-vane wore a coronet with four fleurons. He noted three. Then five. He covered one eye with his hand which smelled faintly of cheese. Then the other. He stood for a spell. Then lowered the blinds, drew the curtains against the spreading light, undressed, and set the alarm for three in the afternoon. There was, he remembered, a meeting.

3

Meetings. How many had he attended in a lifetime? Even his martinet memory could not marshal the lot.

The first, to be sure, remained unforgettable. It took place during the bestial civil war between the Fascist legionnaires, still nesting in their barracks and scouring the blacked-out streets for the partisans, republicans, deserters, fugitives. It had been a clandestine meeting, in the boiler-room of the municipal baths, the building itself having been almost flattened by liberating bombs. He remembered the prickling odour of chlorine and burnt plaster, his father's hacking cough amid the muted voices, and going to bed hungry. His very first political meeting, and his father's defiant pride as they stole home by circuitous alleys and waste ground to the accompaniment of scattered gun-fire out of the thick dark.

Meetings innumerable during his time of probation as messenger and sweeper on the shop-floor: syndical organization, wage protests, strikes, meetings to hear shop stewards and more elevated union officials. There stayed with him the brusque silence of the presses and the drone of oratory by city voices raw with tobacco and lack of sleep. Some time thereafter (he knew the date and hour), baptism: when Tullio took him along to hear a lecture on surplus value in Marxist and Leninist theory. It was delivered by a sweating doctoral student, behind thick glasses whose reflections darted oddly around the brown and green stucco in the packed room. His very first Party meeting. *In memoria*, inviolate, as was also, in that same wild month—the bells had been proclaiming freedom and chewing gum—his first serious experience of sex. More meetings and yet more before he was admitted into that freemasonry of hope. The handshake all around, the austere fever of enlistment, the Party card thrust, with affected calm, into the pocket of his overalls and Tullio's joy at brotherhood within brotherhood.

After that, meetings were legion. Lessons on Marxist social theory, on the heritage of Gramsci, industrialization, the tactics of proletarian protest, the place of women, the media, sport, the arts and sciences, primary and secondary education in a classless state. Films of life in the Soviet Union and analyses of its vanguard destiny. Meetings, obligatory, on Party funding, on the recruitment of new members, on electoral propaganda and discipline, on deviance and factionalism. Sessions devoted to the composition and dissemination of tracts and posters (he was to be made secretary for information and publication). He could remember heated gatherings at the time of the great anti-imperialist, anti-NATO riots and general strikes. Meetings to gather money for comrades with cracked skulls, for the locked-out and the blacklisted. How well he could recall the commemoration, airless, opaquely vibrant as in a sealed chamber, of Stalin's death. They had become orphans huddled in sombre bewilderment. Tullio in tears. A few months later, there had been his only encounter with Togliatti, when he had travelled, with other local delegates and committee members, to the rally and plenary assembly in beflagged, red-draped Bologna. He remembered the leader's sharp smile and the thunder of concordant voices. Meetings at the level of the cell, of the district, of the Party's regional executive so frequent and repetitive that he could no longer distinguish them.

Until the command performance, in the derelict cinema rented for signal occasions, during which he, so frugal of words—for only a written statement can be checked, made intractable to error and false memory—had spoken at length about the evident potential for a fascist resurgence and CIA-financed coup from inside the Hungarian uprising, about the notorious Jew-hatreds of the Cardinal and his White Guard acolytes, about the tragic but unquestionable need (the phrase he actually used was 'dialectical logic') for Soviet intervention. Short of breath but pressing on. The imperialist and plutocratic powers were only waiting for just the tragic, yes, tragic misprision and macabre accident represented by events in Budapest. Witness their actions over the Suez canal. The motion of total solidarity must, therefore, be passed, the complete adherence of the local Party branch to central committee resolutions in Rome must be made manifest.

The pitch of his own voice during that long afternoon and evening stayed with him. As did Tullio's look of desolate love, of a man flayed alive at the moment when his exclusion, together with that of seven other revisionist saboteurs and crypto-Trotskyites, was carried unanimously. Eerily he could hear, as from some archive of echoes within himself, the thud of the baize door as the seven men and the one woman, who was Maura, left the hall.

He had not attended his own ostracism, which came after Prague. Given his intervention during the session called to approve of the Soviet invasion, that ostracism was now as foregone as death itself. Had he not cited Lenin's suppressed testament which revealed the menace posed by Stalinist bureaucracy; had he not adverted to the penitential verities of the Twentieth Party Congress revelations of corruption and the cult of personality; had he not alluded, transparently though without naming him, to Trotsky's model of spontaneous and permanent revolution of the kind, he treacherously inferred, they had witnessed during the Prague Spring? Automatically, the next meeting would be his last. The summons had reached him. Together with the agenda on which his refusal of adequate self-criticism, his violation of Party democracy and discipline, figured amid matters arising.

During what he knew to be the relevant hour he had sat in his room, motionless, made stone. He had sat like a paralytic, his temples pounding as in a cold fever. Knowing that he was being read out of the scroll of the saved, of the elect to hope and meaning. The loneliness of that hour branded him irreparably. It was more solitary than death. He dragged himself to the staircase, intent on going to work, but found himself incapable of useful motion. His legs shook and the nausea made the stair-well spin. He took sick-leave and immured himself in his leprosy. Till Tullio hammered at his door, insistent.

The Circle for Marxist Revolutionary Theory and Praxis numbered less than twenty active members, but met almost as regularly as the Party sections.

And now, as he entered, the props and smells in the schoolroom (made available at nominal cost by the grace of one of the faithful, a primary school teacher), were not much different from those which he had known during his long stay in the belly of the whale.

4

—Tullio.

—*Professore.*

The old, heart-warming joke. Consecrating with that fictive title one whose schooling had been rudimentary but whose physique, with its gaunt concavities, was indeed a touch professorial. More emphatically, that greeting did label a man whose obsessive scruple in respect of the minutiae of print, whose bristling distaste in the face of the approximate and the loosely mistaken, were magisterial and pedantic to a degree.

They shook hands with that hint of mock ceremony which intimate friendship fosters. Handshakes all around, in an aura reassuringly familiar and low-key. Chalk-powder, the odours of scuffed linoleum, the light bulb slightly fugged under its ripped shade. Why, he wondered, were the light bulbs at all such meetings inevitably both grimed with dirt and aggressive, dispensing a yellow, sick-room sheen? Why were the flowers on the desk or podium, even when exalted characters from the regional or national roster came to speak, so waxen? Idle thoughts, when he wanted to concentrate on Anna B.'s report. Comrade Anna. Why his notice of the down, slightly moist, on her upper lip, that hint of a moustache to come?

He tautened and focused on what she was saying.

But the word 'laundromat' kept recurring in so desultory a manner as to make his attention veer. Anna was seeking to analyse the lacunae in classical Marxist social theory revealed by the 'horizontal solidarities' which had developed and coalesced 'spontaneously'—a perilous, crucial adverb—in the working-class high-rise apartment buildings and estates at the new rim of the city. In these solidarities, in the crèches and launderettes, inherited lines of class loyalty and militant activism (Anna's tone was momentarily vibrant), traditional demarcations such as that, for example, between clerk and heavy-goods transporter, were being blurred or frankly eroded.

The dartings to and fro across natural divides of class interest and ideology were, in the main—and Comrade Anna paused slightly—the result of women's clusters. It was the unplanned conviviality of women around the laundromat and the coffee dispenser which wove new alliances and political-social impulses.

The speaker glanced up from her notes. Had anyone, she challenged almost reproachfully, bothered to investigate the radical differences in social infrastructure and peer-group communication as between coffee drawn from, and consumed near, a mechanical dispenser and that brewed in one's own kitchen and poured into one's own cups for a neighbour specifically welcomed and hosted? The new impulses, she reported, were of an essentially consumer-oriented category. This was natural enough and, in its own way, to be welcomed. But the inherent contradictions, the dialectically negative feedback, needed to be understood and fought against. The class struggle in which husbands were inevitably engaged, the combat for better wages, shorter hours and improved safety in the factory were of a kind with which the women, the wives and mothers, found it increasingly difficult to identify. A significant portion of the men and indeed of the women living in the industrial estates were now white-collar, though, to be sure, the percentage among women remained small. These transitional phenomena were, as yet, ill understood. (Too often in his hearing, in his participation in discussions across the long years, had 'ill-understood' been the saving phrase, that which made the suspect or tenebrous visage of the future bearable and the frank insight worth shelving.)

Anna B. went on. There were checkers, counter-personnel, assistant managers at the trucking depot who acted, exactly as Marxist analysis postulated, as parasites on exploited labour. But as their wives mingled with those of the true proletariat on terms of easy intimacy and 'collusive desires'—Anna let this phrase echo, as if in troubled evocation of her own privileged employment as a statistician in the psychiatric social service of the General Clinic—as their daily contacts grew more cohesive, the very concept of the political tended to fade away. What had Marxist and Gramscian sociology to contribute to a better understanding of these 'gender-bonded and gender-oriented socializations'? Had Kautsky or C. Wright Mills said anything to the point?

A certain gloom hung over the Comrade's closing queries. A gloom thickened by the acknowledgement that her untiring efforts to attract even a single potential recruit from the teeming warrens east of the river to the Circle's discussion evenings had failed. Not a single one. He had managed to listen closely. But had he, at a point of especial gravity, caught the imp in Maura's eyes? Was it her bench, that worn school-bench incised to the grain with initials, sobriquets, minor obscenities and arrowed hearts, which had creaked in such irreverent accompaniment to Comrade Anna's report? 'It is necessary to dream' (Lenin, 1902). But not, he reminded himself severely, to day-dream. And at that very moment, Anna having been duly thanked and her most valuable paper having been earmarked for detailed discussion at a later occasion, the members present, ten or eleven in all, turned to him, to the *Professore*, for what had come to be known, in affectionate irony, as the 'homily'. At successive meetings, it was he who glossed the news of the preceding two or three weeks, as culled from *their* newspapers and from *ours*—though no actual newspaper or even review, save a cyclostyled and infrequently distributed bulletin, genuinely reflected the views of the Circle. His commentary drew on eminent foreign papers as well, which his schooled eye sped across in the reading-room of the public library in his *quartiere*, that of Saint Jerome in the Marsh.

What could, what should he say tonight? What must he say if he was to deserve the trust of those now turning towards him (by instinct he always took a seat at the rear)? If Tullio and Maura were to continue being his? He caught himself staring at the wall-map of the nation, as displayed in every schoolroom. He was trying to isolate, among its four colours and infinitely familiar contours, the location of the escarped valley in Sardinia from which came his preferred cheese, the one he had bought and eaten that very day. The island shape was plain enough, as was its capital city in heavy type. But the detail, the recess in which that valley shone, swam before his eyes.

5

News from Prague and the German Democratic Republic, he observed, clearing his throat and bending forward slightly, was indeed difficult to interpret. The facts looked to be undeniable, though dramatized and cheapened by the western media. Thousands were storming embassies, camping at rail-heads and streaming towards the borders. Surface motives were plain enough. The socialist and Marxist regimes had been overtaken by ferocious exasperation, by a breakdown of elementary trust between government and governed. It was worth recalling (he felt the sadness in his bones as he said it) that Gramsci had warned of just such a contingency, of the corrosive fatality of 'family quarrels' in the wake of the Milan and Bologna strikes in the 1920s. But it was the task of the Circle to probe deeper, to lay bare the true nerve of history. The phrase was pompous; he knew it as he heard it out of his own mouth. Could it be that, once again, and in grim similitude to what historians told of the Dark Ages, migrations were thrusting westward out of a deprived, turbulent and inchoate east?

—What about the cars?

Cesare Lombardi's interruption arrested his train of thought.

—Cars?

—They are abandoning their cars. Thousands of them. They are dumping them at the frontiers or giving them away. I've seen it on television. Men and women kicking their cars and leaving them in the ditch.

Friend Lombardi did have a gift for angular queries. He launched his circuitous darts from a stooped posture, eyes downcast, perspiring behind his tortoiseshell glasses.

—I know that. (Patiently.)

Lombardi breathed heavily. He chain-smoked, as if the hunger he had traversed during the last years of the war, when he crawled from lair to lair in fear of denunciation as a half-Jew and known anarchist, had never left him.

—Their cars are miserable. It is said you can smell their exhaust for miles. But imagine abandoning them. Just like that!

He warmed to his theme, gathering it in like a faintly repulsive quarry.

—I ask you: why do they have all those foul machines in the first place? Polluting, wasting raw materials, consuming fossil fuels. It's pure lunacy. As bad as capitalism. Worse. When we know that bicycles will do for ninety per cent of our actual daily needs. That bicycles are clean and silent. And that a proper public transport system can provide for the rest. Those hordes of stinking cars by the roadside. Don't you see what that really means? It makes no difference whether we live over here or over there. Even the worst of those automobiles (the epithet which Lombardi appended was an old-fashioned, eroded obscenity) is totally beyond the reach of the Third World. Imagine what a doctor in Angola or Peru or China would give for even one of those Trabants. For the energy they consume, a useless dream, I know (the point of his cigarette drew an angry arc) but one which hundreds of millions of human beings in Africa, Asia and Latin America would pay for. Every bloody and killing day of their wretched existence. Can you imagine what these men and women feel when they see those pictures of junked, abandoned cars and homes and jobs? There can be no life worth living on this pillaged earth, no justice worth having so long as . . .

Lombardi paused to draw breath.

—Your analyses make me ill. Don't you see? We must learn to make do. Each and every one of us. With essentials. Using our legs to walk or pedal. Baking one decent sort of bread and not ten cellophane kinds. Our forests are going to pulp because there are a hundred—or is it more?—girlie magazines on the kiosks. We fly half-empty jumbos to cities already served by a dozen other airlines. Now cars are being littered by the side of the road like used Kleenex. To each according to his needs. Blessed Karl Marx! Does no one remember what real needs are? How few. How richly they could be satisfied? Superfluity enslaves. We have gone mad with superfluity. In the shanty-town of Rio or Soweto—have you seen those television pictures?—families try to stay alive under bits of corrugated tin and rubber, next to open cesspits. Every one of those tossed away Trabants could shelter . . .

His incensed delivery failed him. Being corpulent, addicted to nicotine, a tireless collector of vintage jazz records and memorabilia, Cesare Lombardi, telephone engineer by profession, harboured a burning predilection for images of asceticism, for ideals of saintly privation. He dreamt of the Desert Fathers, of the Stylites, naked to the winds on their pillars of denial.

Father Carlo Tessone, sitting at an angle to him, knew this. Father Carlo, their only comrade from the Church, though his status was, for some time, marginal. He, evidently, was a man who did not find it difficult to make do, to stay thin, to walk the city in his one patched garb and mended, high-laced boots. A self-denier with amused eyes and a touch of courtliness in his spare gestures.

Now Father Carlo spoke softly.

—Lombardi, to hear you one might think that Marxism must arrive at deprivation. That a just, proletarian distribution of resources and of the means of production is, after all, a sort of monasticism in the barrens. A clerisy of abstinence.

Father Carlo let this elegant phrase fall with a hint of

embarrassment. He had, he knew, a weakness for eloquence. No abnegation there but the old schooling at the seminary in rotundity and rhetoric.

The *Professore* realized he must take the reins.

—Yes. This is one of the charges brought against us. Against all Marxist models. That ours are the politics and institutions of backwardness. I remind those present here of the debates on this very issue in Plekhanov and Veblen. Is Marxism at bottom a strategy for survival in underdeveloped or stagnant economies, is it inherently alien to material progress and consumer-oriented social structures? When it is, so manifestly, a product, an analytic science, a discovery of historical laws, sprung of the industrial revolution and of the expansion of planetary resources?

Tullio interjected. His tone was oddly neutral, which made his question the more ominous.

—*Professore*: those East German Trabants. Why should they be so undesirable? Why can a Marxist economy, in a country with a history of industrial strength and a skilled work-force, not produce a satisfactory internal combustion engine and chassis? Isn't that the real question?

Further voices chimed in. The discussion eddied. It was inconclusive and, at times, ill-tempered.

He had to get to work. Outside the unwashed windows, the bells had sounded vespers. It was agreed that the questions raised would be further argued as events unfolded in the east. Leaving—renewed handshakes and the shuffling on of raincoats —he noted Maura's nod. It was, he judged, imperceptible to anyone else. It signalled Sunday.

6

Weather permitting, they met at the end-station of the tramline in Via Alba. Then took the rackety train which looped the hill towns and villages to the north of the city. Maura brought the sandwiches and the fruit. The coffee thermos and bottle of wine were his responsibility. Sometimes he felt lavish and added cheese or a jar of olives. Without any particular destination in mind, they would alight at one or another of the small stations, punch the gravel with their walking-sticks and head upward. In the past, Tullio had quite often come along; once or twice Lombardi had puffed in their wake. Even Anna B. had been of the party, blushing at her hob-nailed, sensible boots and tight trousers. But not of late. Maura and he had become, so distinctly, a couple.

The air was soft with October's end but had in it the uncertain light of the coming rains. Traversing the village, they passed the door, left ajar, of the church, and heard the muffled echoes of mass. Soon the cracked voice of the single bell would chime briefly to the hills. They took the goat-track which meandered skyward through the laurel, the thorn-bushes and the fallow strips of stubble, scratched as if with bare hands and blackened nails out of the jumble of rocks.

The valley fell away quickly. Turning back he and Maura could see, even of a Sunday, the dun scarf of pollution unwound across the city and the new industrial zones. But here, above the dozen rust-tinted roofs of Verzzani (they had noted the name on the station-master's hut), the folds of air shook softly as the last of the summer winds sang past, bound southward, he fancied, to nest and noise in the broken barns, in the almost spectral, bleached hamlets from which migrant labour was now pressing north. And as in rebound to his thought, a train-whistle shrilled in the valley, on the main line, with its third-class carriages ferrying the uprooted and the bewildered to the slums of the cities.

He drew a long breath, saw Maura's lithe back rounding a turn in the trail just above him, and inhaled a faint trace of thyme. Soon now the sun would top the ridge and Maura would pause to strip off her jumper, knotting it around her hips under the rucksack.

It was she, roughly ten yards ahead of him, who, shading her smoke-grey eyes, pointed to a hollow in the overhanging screed. The very recent first autumn rains and gusts of colder wind had splayed the bushes. Something whitish and shaped shone in the little dell. They cut to the left through barbed grass. His metal-tipped cane struck a fallen, flat piece of stone paving. The impact rang bright. Other stone fragments lay near under the overhang of rock and tufa. Barely visible in the tangle of heather and striated chalk stood a small column, its fluting encrusted with lichen. Maura gave a low, cheery cry. The carved stone was cracked and at an angle. But her fingers could trace remnants of lettering. They knelt side by side. The air was still and warm in that hollow place. Minutely, he began brushing the mud and the lighter shards of rubble and crystallized rock from the graven lines. Maura turned to him inquiringly. He caught the nearness of her cheek and the embers in her hair. She was not, he supposed, beautiful. Only so much more than that.

They had, he proposed, chanced on one of the numerous miniature shrines or modest family memorials which dotted these hills. He added, with a pedantry which at once amused and embarrassed him, that these dated from the palaeo-Christian period, at the ebb-tide of the decomposing Roman empire, when Christendom flourished in the silent places. This site must, he ruled, be marked on the fifty-metre scale archaeological survey in the *Museo municipale*.

Now he extracted the large old-style handkerchief from his pocket (Maura always smiled at the gesture) and began cleaning the incisions. He blew neatly at the detritus and cleared the thin branches that had made their bed of the antique marble. Maura's shoulder warmed his arched back.

The text was fractured and eroded nearly beyond supposition. It ran between shallow double-borders and a motif, perfunctorily carved, which might, he guessed, be acanthus leaf. In one of the whorls a snail had left its indelible mark. Hurried labour, he reflected, the work of unskilled or hunted hands using, almost certainly, an earlier pagan site and votive stone for their urgent purpose.

—How can you be so sure that this is a Christian marker or inscription?

Instinct. He might be wrong. But his fingers read the chiselling, the style of the letters as fourth-century, late third at the earliest. And although he could not be confident of making out correctly the roughened, largely effaced emblem, he could swear it was that of a fish, crudely drawn, between two stars. The symbol of the Son of God, the contours of resurrection so common in early Christian lapidaries and cult objects.

—*M*, said Maura.

—And *N*. I can't make out the letter in between.

His fingers passed and repassed delicately over the lost braille.

—*E* and *T*. He spelt out the two letters with assurance.

—*MANET*. And in this buried spot, the sun now full above them, his voice boomed. For he was certain of his reading.

The words, following only edges and the remembrance of scoured angles and curves which worked stone retains across time, could be guessed at. But he had little doubt. The rotundity of the *O* was live to his thumb. No hand or eye acquainted with the serration characteristic of the stem of the capital *R* in the early Christian or late Roman stone-carver's alphabet could mistake the word or, more precisely, its certain shadow.

—*AMOR*. He spoke the four letters with gentle triumph.

—*MANET AMOR*. Love remains. Love endures.

—You are making it up, whispered Maura, but repeated the Latin.

—The name must have been on the upper half of the tablet. A child's name, I think. Given the size of the stone. A child gone. Here, in these hills. When the family was under way, perhaps. Fleeing, or just crossing the col to join another community. A Lavinia, a Drusilla, of whom love remains.

—It could just as well have been a little boy, objected Maura.

He nodded, and his heart drummed.

She asked: Ought we to have uncovered it?

—The rains did that. And the winds.

—They did not read the words. If we found a letter fallen on the road, would we read it?

—This letter, Maura, was meant for us.

He felt awkward at the sound of his own intensity, hearing in that banality the hunger. But she nodded lightly and smiled. They rose to their feet. She peeled off her sweater and looked about for a moment. They propped their sacks and sticks against the warming stone. Again, he tasted a touch of thyme in the air and the secret scent of lavender late in the parting year. He half-closed his eyes so as to take in fully the brush of her clothes as she slipped out of her jersey and hiking pants. She glided her arms behind her back and he could hear the hooks open. The ground was strange under his feet. When he stretched beside her, she was naked.

7

He had long given television a wide berth. After the night's proof-reading it was sensible to give his eyes all possible rest. The afternoon programmes, which he could have switched on, were, he knew, trash: housewives' strip-tease, family quiz shows and morose comedians out of the hinterland. Maura's insistence that they should install themselves in front of the little screen on that late November Sunday evening had irritated and disturbed him. Now he sat mesmerized.

Father Carlo had joined them. There was no television in the broom-closet of a room which he occupied fitfully at the hostel. He had brought a bag of macaroons, of which the *Professore* was inordinately fond. The grit of almonds and burnt sugar clung happily to one's teeth. The padre too was spellbound, hunched forward on the kitchen stool, so compact in his observance of the screen that his weight and occasional shuffle seemed shadowy.

The titles, credits and presenter's overture had been breathless. Pictures, action sequences, interviews, exclusive documentary footage would be shown over the next two hours to mark 'the greatest wave of revolution, the greatest blossoming of freedom history had ever known.' There would be expert commentaries from Minister X, Professor Y and novelist Z. They would, in turn, join a panel assembling further luminaries of the political spectrum and of sociology. As the celebrated compère spoke, his mouth an almost perfect *O* of bounteous excitement, bursts of Beethoven rising on the sound-track, and the chorale of the Ninth proceeded towards the fiercely spotlit Brandenburg Gate.

First came the Berlin saga and the crumbling of the Wall.

Once again, the screen showed a wave of humanity pouring through. Border guards grinned vacantly and reached for cigarettes as do the bears in a bankrupt circus. Shots of teenagers from the east tumbling into West Berlin supermarkets, rocking in wonder before the shelves, emptying them in a sleep-walker's sweep. Bright-tinted toothpaste, lacquer for toe-nails, soft toilet-paper in the hues of the rainbow, deodorants, tights finely meshed and stippled, jeans bleached or mended. Sun-glasses for the night, amplifiers, cassettes, coffee beans from Brazil being whipped off the shelves and display cases. The reporter's lens and microphone homed in on a bounding, guffawing troupe, their carrier-bags piled high with video cassettes and sun-bright plastic rain-wear. One of the lads mouthed his message straight into the bobbing mike: 'Horror-films, man. Porno. Hot lips, man.' And the girls in his wake screeched with joy and did a twist on the pavement. The camera swung back to the Wall itself and to the idle bulk of the Gate. Politicians embraced. A film star (minor) signed autographs on the platform of a watch-tower. At every instant, the throng grew larger and more torrential.

Cut, and over to 'our colleague in Prague.' The bells pealing across unkempt gables. Havel on the balcony. 'Freedom . . . nation . . . democracy.' Eyes misted, the whirlpools of sudden laughter and tears in the crowd, the voices echoing from group to group, from parade to parade, the multitude at once empowered and set free. Newsreel shots of Soviet tanks in 1968, on the exact same street-corners where the Czechs now stood in recollection and soft drunkenness as if the very wind, clanging with bells, were alcohol.

The ads rolled on. Then Warsaw and Gdánsk. A gross memorial to the Soviet liberators of 1944–45 being toppled into a cloud of brown dust. Brief collages of the death-ditches at Katyn, of Stalinist edifices against a sullen sky. Then the early images of Solidarity, of that walrus-man with the obstinate eyes and slow triumphs. An interview with a foreman outside a steel-mill: 'We have nothing left. We must begin again at zero. They stole everything. Communist bandits. Filth.' Close-up of his bony face, of hands sandpapered like those of the unfed in some African drought.

The first of the pundits, in a professorial study. 'Yes. He agreed entirely. An earthquake. Promethean. The liberation of the human spirit from the shackles of Marxist-Leninist folly and despotism. May I emphasize "Leninist"? You will be so good as to recall, *cara* Valeria' (the interviewer nodded supportively) 'the book in which I pointed out, many years ago, oh the clairvoyance and confidence of one's youth, that so-called "Stalinism" is nothing more than an ineluctable development, I stress "ineluctable", my dear friends, of the homicidal Leninist, indeed Marxist, blueprint.' At which pronouncement, the camera glided tastefully behind the sage's brow to show a panorama of the Milan skyline.

Now back to the action. To a meeting of the Hungarian Democratic Centre. Demands for the immediate withdrawal of Soviet forces. Immediate. Pictures of the walled-in barracks on the outskirts of Budapest, of women and children shaking their fists at Red Army sentries, teenagers with glazed faces and cheap plastic gun-belts. A capsule-chat with the new Minister of the Interior. 'We do have the infrastructure here in Budapest. Remember our illustrious economists. But help is needed. Urgently. Investment, *Signor*, and more investment. As I told my friend Andreotti, democracy costs money. In this whole building there is hardly a phone left that works. Not a single fax-machine at my disposal!' Arms outflung in quixotic despair and resolution.

'We are taking you to Sofia. Exclusive.' The presenter's vibrato rose. 'Pictures not seen before. A people on the march.' Fields. A file of men, women and children in embroidered blouses following a flower-decked tractor. A village hall. Editorial apologies for the quality of the sound. A large man, his braces sweated through, yelling into a small loud hailer. Something about the price of oats and those Bolshevik locusts in Sofia. The assembly in responsion: 'Down with the Communists. Zhivkov to the lantern.'

A second break for ads. Motor-scooters circling a house-high Jeroboam of alcohol-free champagne. 'Safety bubbles,' crooned the young woman, her adam's apple pulsing ecstatically.

The round table, which was to crown the programme, had

harvested politicians, more professors, the winner of this season's stellar prize for fiction (was the man lightly rouged?).

'Oh, there could be no doubt. No shadow of a doubt. History had turned on its hinges. The nightmare of state-socialism was lifting. It was plain as daylight: Marxism had led to the Gulag and the massacres at Timisoara. To the extermination and enslavement of millions. To those cunning falsehoods which had suborned and infected western sensibility.' ('Sensibility' dropped subtly from the novelist's pursed lips and was taken up in caressing counterpoint by the eminent psychologist.)

Communism? *Finis*. Only Cuba, Yemen and Albania—but Albania for how much longer?—left in red on the world map. 'An unholy trinity, dear colleagues and treasured spectators.' Decorous mirth around the tinkling water-bottles. The evident problem was Russia itself. How long before it broke into pieces, its deprived millions trudging westward? How long before the Baltic republics, the vast Ukraine, Armenia, Georgia, Uzbekistan, little Moldavia, Siberia itself (who could foretell?) declared their independence from the impotent centre?

The bald historian urged caution: 'These seismic movements take time. Russian patriotism . . . the hydrogen bomb and space-programme. After all . . .'

But the syndicated columnist tugged impatiently at his bow-tie and offered wagers to all participants: 'The USSR will collapse within eighteen months. There will be anarchy when the soldiers come home. Pogroms. Bread riots. Yeltsin is ready to make his move. I have it on highest authority. From the horse's mouth, believe me! Within a year and a half. Perhaps less. *Kaput*.' And he passed his hand across his windpipe, the heavy signet-ring glinting.

The moderator turned brusquely to Comrade Gabrielli of the Central Committee in Rome. 'Well, *Dottore*?'

A final bouquet of ads. To maintain suspense. To prepare the audience for revelation.

Why was Gabrielli ill-shaven?

'We are, as you know, committed to a multi-party democracy. We have been for a long time. Even Togliatti . . . This present crisis . . . how shall I put it?'

He lunged at the television and stabbed at the switch. Neither Father Carlo nor Maura moved. The sofa, the book-shelves, the stool brought in from the kitchen, lay in darkness. He glanced at the plants in the window-box. Their leaves hung motionless. Rubbery. Maura turned on the table-lamp (it had been his first gift to her) and brought coffee. Father Carlo stretched and massaged his thin back.

Leaving, the *Professore* almost tripped over the door-sill.

Maura caught his elbow: You must see the eye doctor. You *must*.

She had urged it under her breath, but Carlo, who had preceded him down the murky stairs, turned and looked back.

8

—Not for this!

He heard himself repeating the phrase. The pink and yellow flashes from the window display of the all night video-rental shop made his cheeks clown-like and his eyes blink.

Father Carlo grinned at him.

—Careful, *Professore*. That's been *our* line. Not for *this* world. Not for the filth and lucre and beatings of this life. There must be something better. Since that day when they drove the nails into his hands and feet. There just has to be something beyond bread and circuses.

Father Carlo's cadence seemed to mime and tease his own.

—It would be unbearable if it had all been only for this. As you say, old friend. All that pain, the dirt up to our eyeballs. If this turned out to be the be all and end all, the sum total, we would do best to hang ourselves on the next lamp-post. On the next meat hook. When the great white dawn didn't come and set Galilee or Samaria alight, there were those who did hang themselves or pitch themselves head first into wells. They had seen the black sun on his dead eyes, on his torn flesh. All for nothing. So they did away with themselves. Many did it again when the year one thousand came and went, with the usual rain and the customary plagues and the ordinary famines. And they'll do it again, on the first common morning of the year two thousand. Shouting: 'Not for this! It's been too long. How can it all have been only for this? The promise and the desolation.'

Father Carlo continued: That's where we came in. The mother Church. With the aspirin. Gently now, good children. Don't swallow too fast. Let it melt in your mouths. Wrap it in a wafer. Wash it down with a sip of wine. Gently. For it is his body and watery blood. Spilt for you, and now within you. The pain-killer. So that you can endure. Till Sunday week. In your garbage lives, in your hunger and lice, in the incontinence of the geriatric ward or that of the new-born cretins. Just another little week to crawl through. Till the next medication. Let the promise fill your empty bellies. His kingdom will come. Not quite yet, not here in any real sense, but without fail: in the tomorrow after tomorrow's tomorrow.

—Observe our mercies. Do not rage at injustice, at the wealth flung in your face, at the torture of the innocent and the helpless. Do not lament your own misery. Do not bare your broken teeth against your children's hunger. These are but passing trials. Bear them meekly. Give the slaughterhouse men a smile, bow to the rich, cast down your eyes when the depraved roar past. Theirs may be the rewards here and now. Yours are yet to come. Acknowledge the cunning of my text. Order and obeisance in this vale of sorrows, compensation over there. Around the next corner of time.

He had listened, his chin against the raised collar of his coat: Do you know what socialism is, reverend Father? Do you know what it really is?

Father Carlo turned to him lightly: What is it, my friend? What is it really?

—It is impatience. Impatience. That's what socialism is. A rage for now.

And the spurt in his voice made him sound hoarse.

Father Carlo nodded: So it was in early Christianity. Exactly so. Impatience ran wild in Jesus. When he cursed the pitiful fig-tree, or when he said that he had come bearing a sword. Or when he bade the dead bury their dead or when he rushed into

Jerusalem unprepared and ran riot in the Temple yard. His impatience may well have been more terrible than that suffered by any other living being. He was so impatient to enter into the mystery of his own beginning and become what he was. And what did Christ leave his little mafia? A treasure of impatience. They panted for the end of time like dogs dying of thirst. For the last sunset. They believed it to be imminent, a week away, a month at most. They smelled the huge rank smell of the end. They thought they saw the seals breaking on the book of life. But it didn't come to pass, did it? Or it came and passed by like snow at midnight, unnoticed. History had not pulled down the shutters. And we were back on the treadmill. Whereupon the Church ordered patience and more patience, and handed out tranquillizers.

He laughed almost joyously: But you see there have been quite a few among us who never learned the arts of waiting. Heresy also is impatience. The heretic takes short cuts. We too have had our dreamers of tomorrow. Justice for everyman, as Jesus wanted. Peace upon earth. No more swollen bellies and flies on starved children. To each according to his needs. No, much more: to each according to his dignity and aspirations. Tomorrow at daybreak. Or, at the very latest, Monday next.

—How effectively the Church has dealt with the impatient ones. The millenarians, the mendicants, the anabaptists, the Adamites, the Brethren of True Love, all the crazed preachers of a new Jerusalem! How it has scourged and erased them from history. Not a single text left of the Cathars, who taught perfection here and now. There is nothing Rome has dreaded more than impatience. His kingdom is not of this world. Has there ever been a more adroit political manifesto? Tell me, *Professore*.

The two walkers found themselves looking at each other and so nearly in step.

—It is not only you socialists who have been impatient. Some of us have been pretty well mad with impatience, *mio caro*. For so long. But what earthly use has it been?

Father Carlo stumbled over his own word. He took it up a second time with a chuckle.

—Earthly. That's the whole point, isn't it? Of what use has it been here *on earth*? How impatient Jesus must have been in that tomb. Three days can be a very long time. A small eternity. For us it's been longer.

They had left the Corso. Unnoticing, they headed towards the river.

—Much longer.

They crossed puddles of thicker blackness where the high, nailed-over portals of condemned palaces and tenements cast their night shadows.

Father Carlo was humming. A vacant, up down tune. The hum of the Psalmist or of the half-woken monk in the chill of matins.

They caught the scent of the river. Tar and wisps of diesel.

—We did take that impatience from you. I know that, Carlo. But you were not the first. The hunger is much older. The rage was in Moses. The commandments of justice were his and the abstentions. Those endless inventories of what it is we must do without. Moses knew he couldn't enter the promised land. It would be too small for his fury.

—Have you read Amos, *reverendissime*? Only communists now read the Bible. Amos was out of his mind with anger. At the greed which parades through the cities, at the empty eyes of the child beggars. All our impatience since seems to me like an echo of his voice. He knew. He knew the world in which grain is burned or rat-poisoned so that prices do not fall on the commodities exchange and in which children are sold on the night streets or set to labour in carpet factories and bead-shops, fourteen hours at a stretch, till they go blind and tubercular. Amos had seen it all. He had heard the giggle of money and stepped in its vomit. And Jesus after him, I agree. 'There shall come a time when men will exchange love for love, justice for justice.' Not lucre for lucre, Carlo? Was it an Evangelist? Was it Saint Francis or Mother Teresa? Tell me, Father Carlo, who prophesied thus? Marx did. Karl Marx. In 1844. When he was writing to and for himself. Putting impatience to paper. Not strategy or analysis or polemic. But prophecy and promise out of a great rage. The very beard of that man was angry.

They had come on to the bridge.

Carlo's move: Moses and the Prophets. The man from Nazareth. Marx. Just as the Nazis said. Communism is Judaism writ large, the virus of Bolshevism is the Jew-virus.

They were leaning over the wrought-iron balustrade, enamelled with pigeon droppings. His nails scraped idly at the stuff. Would Father Carlo, he wondered, perform the stock gesture out of morose French movies. Father Carlo did. The match flared and arched from his fingers into the slow current below.

—I don't know much about Jews. I was young when it was done to them. But I have my own theory. That business about being a chosen people, the covenant with history. I believe in it. But not in the way they tell it, Father Carlo: it is the wretched who are chosen. It is those who are born into hunger, into AIDS. It is the congenitally deformed and the deaf-mutes. It is almost the whole cursed lot of us. The numberless tribe of the losers. God chose us to be those who wait. Till our waiting will grow so unendurable that justice and brotherhood must explode out of us. Have you ever looked closely at those waiting for the soup-kitchens to open, for the blankets they hand out in the doss house? They only *seem* like the dead. Look closer. Behind their eyes, a long dark way behind, the embers are alive. The thorn-bush is burning inside them. They are the chosen people of despair. But also of hope, Carlo.

He had veered towards him, full-face: What the hell can a rich man hope for? Why bother with hope when your belly is full? That's what makes every victim a Jew, a real Jew. The truly chosen do not descend from Abraham, who was a millionaire. We do not come from Job, who doubled his holdings. We are the children of Hagar. We have fed on stones, and wasps have sung for us. There can be no communist, no real socialist who is not, at bottom, a Jew.

A string of barges, their lights reddish, passed underneath. The arches of the bridge resounded to the coughing motors.

As he stared at the receding lights, conviction quite

overcame him: Do listen to me, Carlo. It sounds silly. But here is how I see it. When a man or woman is made an outcast, when they humiliate and spit at us, whoever we are, wherever we may be, we become Jews. In that instant.

—A dark syllogism, *Professore*. Look where it led.

—But that's the whole point. Don't you see? The Jews refused to take the promissory note. To swallow what you call aspirin. They saw that nothing had changed after Jesus. Men ate men, just as before. Beggars remained beggars. So he could not be the Messiah, could he? Not the one worth waiting for, whose true coming would make a lit place of the world. Now and for ever.

Father Carlo let a second match flare in his cupped hand and watched its descending glow, but said nothing.

—It does make sense, surely you see that? There were Jews who saw deeper and understood that the Messiah would never come. Never. Or rather, that the Messiah was man himself. That the revelation and the great winds to come were those of our own history. That ordinary men and women had not even begun to *be themselves*.

He exulted at the obviousness of it.

—Men and women, creatures of reason, custodians of this earth: yes, there is a Messiah and a Jerusalem but not after one's funeral and not out of pink clouds. And there are laws, but not ones spewed out of some volcano in Sinai. There are laws of history, and science, and supply and demand. And if you need miracles, look around you! At the irrigation of a desert, at the finding of penicillin, at the invention of braille, at the ability of simple algebra to fix the exact location of a star a hundred million light years away. So many miracles that it's embarrassing. Why turn water into wine—any village conjuror can do that—when you can turn rags into paper and lead into print?

He was talking too much. Orating. Pontificating as if in some third-rate allegoric novel. He flushed at the heat of his own voice. When he knew that talk came cheap, that his only true craft was that of silent print, which could be corrected, checked and checked again. Chattering away like one on the threshold of drunkenness.

They fell into step and crossed to the eastern quarters of the city. These had their own night hum. When Father Carlo turned to him they were on a flight of damp steps from the embankment to the tramlines and to one of the tunnel-dark alleys which led from the river to Piazza San Severo.

—Miracles?

Father Carlo had made the word sound sadder than any other in the language, and grimier.

—The miracles of reason and the laws of history? I don't know about you, *Professore*, but I can just about picture to myself, say, a thousand people. In a hall. Or, vaguely, a few thousand in a stadium. A figure like one million means nothing to me. I can't get any purchase on it. Twenty-five million. That we are told was the number of men, women and children Stalin starved, froze, tortured to death. Twenty-five. I can say the number but can grasp nothing of its reality, of its concrete meaning. So I focus on one single human being. On a nun they arrested for counter-revolutionary attitudes and sabotage some time in 1937. They transported her to Kolyma, to the Arctic Circle. In the hold that took prisoners from Vladivostok to the mines, on one of those hell barges, she begged and screamed for water. They pissed in her mouth, asked her whether it was as tasty as communion wine, and raped her. She was then told to make neat mounds of the earth and stones being hauled out of the shafts. The women had only a kind of raw shift to wear. In the summer many went mad, literally mad, with mosquito bites and swamp fever. Sister Evgenia lived into the winter. One day there was so little light on the tundra that she piled the stones without due care. They toppled over. She was beaten, on and off, for ten hours. Then she was sent back to pile them up again. No sleep allowed her. When she passed out, they poured ice water over her and made her stand to attention in the puddle. Her feet froze to the ground. Burning more horribly than in fire. Sister Evgenia stood there through the whole day. We have eye-witnesses. First she said out loud, 'May God forgive you.' Over and over. Then she crooned prayers and begged the Holy Mother to intercede for those who had beaten her. That evening the other women in the labour-squad had to chop down her body with an axe. Her eyes were still open.

—So I do my best to make Sister Evgenia stand for 24,999,999 other human beings done to hopeless death by your miracles! By your proud winds of history and scientific laws of social progress. I can't manage it. No brain can comprehend what your fine freedom did to man on this planet. There is not, just now, dear friend, a day when they are not digging up mass graves in the forests of the Ukraine, skulls by the ten thousands, each with a neat little bullet-hole in its back, skeletons, their wrists bound with wire so that the pain would grow worse till the moment of execution. That's what came of your Messiah for man. A savagery beyond understanding. Mass-murder which makes the soul sick when one even tries to think of it. Arise ye prisoners of starvation. Oh yes: so that we can push you into the lime-pits. Break your chains. So we can flog you to death with them. Red dawn in the east. Light by which to kill and maim and reduce to cringing terror the millions of coolies from Beijing to Prague, from Kolyma to the Turkestan desert. As you say: they did irrigate those deserts. With blood. And there was penicillin: for the killers and court-jesters. Why, indeed, turn water into wine? A paltry trick, I agree. When you can turn human blood and human sweat into gold and iron-ore.

Father Carlo flung the question at him as out of some huge distance though they had kept the same pace. The narrow alley, with its rare, stove-in lamps hooked to the tenement walls, rang with their voices.

—Stalin was trained in a seminary. He was taught damnation and the blessed necessity of hell and had behind him a thousand years of anathema, of church despotism and censorship. Who has massacred more consistently than the churches?

Carlo interrupted, flaring: For pity's sake. Not that old saw again. The Inquisition and Galileo. Even a novice dialectician could do better than that! Do you honestly believe that I don't know what suffering, what destruction the churches have caused? Do you imagine there is a day when I don't remember that Jew-hatred and the hounding of the so-called heretic sprang from the very first roots of Christianity, and feel sick to my soul? Can you believe that I would be with you tonight, *mio caro*, or be one of the faithful in our pitiful Marxist coven if I didn't know all that and worse?

At the word 'coven' they both laughed loud and loosened. They had entered the trim square with its fountain. Undersized obelisks encircling nymphs and sea-horses rotund and decrepit in their immemorial thirst. Odd, he reflected, how the ring and plash of a fountain is different at night-time. More subterranean, somehow. A chill blew from the plumes of water and he tightened his scarf.

—But there is a difference.

The emeritus priest said it calmly: A cardinal difference, if you will allow the term. The crimes of the churches have been committed in the name of a revealed, transcendent verity. The fires were no less hot or the censorship less suffocating. I know that. On that level, there can be no apologia. But those who did these hideous things were labouring to save souls. They were betting on eternity. They held themselves, poor cruel imbeciles, to be God's agents. The stakes were so high, so pure and free of earthly benefit, that any sin would be a crime, an uncaring without end. But at the heart of communism there is a demeaning of man and woman worse than the tyrannies and depravities in Christendom, foul as these are.

Father Carlo stopped, fixed for an instant in his own perception: At the heart of communism is the lie. The central, axiomatic lie: a kingdom of justice, a classless brotherhood, a release from servitude here and now. In this world. That's the great lie. The systematic bribing and betraying of human hope. The perversion is monstrous. To turn war into the word 'peace', a continent of slave-labour into the motherland of socialist freedom. For seventy measureless years that perversion made human beings tremble in their rooms like trapped animals, rewrote history according to the lunatic whims of the despot, rubbed out the names of the executed and the banished so that memory itself—memory, *Professore*—would be emptied of truth, like a garbage-bin. So that the names could not be made a prayer. Sister Evgenia. Sister Evgenia of the frozen feet. Just speak it with me this once. She will hear us. She and the erased ghosts butchered not in the name of grace everlasting, but so that gangsters and hangmen and bureaucrats could fatten. Corruption without end. The lie in every nerve. What your scientific state-socialism produced was not even Satan's realm as the apocalyptics and the inquisitors foresaw it. It was something smaller, tawdrier, more inhuman. Like a world ruled by poisonous lice. Your earthly messiahs turned out to be nothing but hypocritical hoodlums. Lords of lice.

At the corner of the wider street was an all-night café, harshly lit. The steamed urns with their crowned tops and silvery sheen reminded Father Carlo of Torah scrolls he had seen in an exhibition of Jewish remnants. The thump of the juke-box could be heard even in the street, but as if muted by the dead hour. Its tired cadence blended with the beat of the fountain as it receded behind them. Sugary crumbs and rolls gone hard (the bakeries would open in about an hour) clung to the glass bells on the formica table-tops. But the coffee was hot and they cradled it in their hands. Father Carlo went back to the counter and bought two glasses of *strega*. He set them down cautiously, brimful. From across the room, under the calendar of the *Mundial*, now sacred history, a woman flashed the two men a companionable leer.

—But now, Carlo? What now?

—*What then shall we do?*' A fine title. Lenin's best book. Written when he was powerless. An exile. What you would call 'a Jew'.

—Consider the source of our error. Of that great lie. And mark you, I don't accept that it was. Or that there were only venal butchers at the top. Consider.

Momentarily, he held the coffee in his mouth. It was good coffee, but as he swallowed and let the dusky heat seep through him, a greater tiredness seemed to follow.

—Marxism did man supreme honour. The Moses and Jesus and Marx vision of the just earth, of a neighbour's love, of human universality, the abolition of barriers between lands, classes, races, the abolition of tribal hatreds: *that* vision was—we've agreed, haven't we?—a huge impatience. But it was more.

It was an overestimate of man. A possibly fatal, possibly deranged but none the less magnificent, jubilant overestimate of man. The highest compliment ever paid him. The Church has held man in doleful contempt. He is a fallen creature, doomed to sweat out his life-sentence. Dust to dust. Marxism has taken him to be almost boundless in his capacities, limitless in his horizons, in the leaps of his spirit. A reacher to the stars. Not mired in original sin, but himself original. Our history is nothing but a savage prologue.

—A true Bolshevik, Carlo, owns nothing but the clothes on his back. No home. No family. No forgiveness if he breaches discipline or makes a mistake. Listen to me carefully: *he does not even have hope*. Not in your sense. No lilies and incense to come. No mass said for his dead soul. He has something more unyielding than hope, more worthy of man's unmapped intellect and guts. The right words are hard to find. He has *insight*.

He said it twice over.

—He understands his own condition and necessary suffering. He knows what defeat tastes like and even passing despair. There are 40,000 communards, men, women, twelve-year-old boys, buried in mass graves under the shopping-streets of Paris. The hopes of a communist are a way of seeing with absolute clarity. Exactly as through a radio-telescope which brings us the facts about a universe infinitely older than the human race and which will evolve long after our extinction. Such seeing is clearer than hope. It honours man beyond every honour. That's where we went wrong.

—And never forget, *padre*, that there *have been* men and women, and more than just a handful, who have lived up to the expectations of Marxism, who have *lived up*! Rosa Luxemburg when they clubbed her to death or the volunteers in the International Brigade or Gramsci, here, among us or the communist partisans silent under torture. All deceived. But were they deceived? Who gave what medical aid they could in the starving villages, and kept faith in the Gulag, as your nun did, and died praising Stalin, knowing even in their own insane misery, that it was he who had made Russia capable of withstanding the fascist onslaught. Mankind is not made up of saints and martyrs. It is not made up of those drunk with justice and possessed by reason. Yes, we got it wrong. Hideously wrong, as you say. But the big error, the overestimate of man from which the mistake came, is the single most noble motion of the human spirit in our awful history. To me, to so many before me, it has compensated for our failings. It has made of that drunken slut over there something without limits. Every beggar is a prince of possibility.

Father Carlo saluted the formula: You *are* a dialectician, old friend. Your health!

The *strega* went down like brown flame.

They took a second glass, and his hand shook a little as he brushed Carlo's sleeve.

—Capitalism never made that mistake. Don't you see? The free market takes man at his mean average. And mean is the word. It invests in his animal greed. It makes a balance sheet of his egotism and his petty interests. It caresses his appetites for goods and comforts and mechanical toys and holidays in the sun. Tickling his belly so that he rolls over and begs for more. Which keeps consumerism going. Capitalism has not left man where it found him; it has lessened him. We are become a pack snarling for luxuries, grunting at the trough. That second car. A larger refrigerator. We are indeed possessed, more so than any of the crazed and the demonic in your manuals of witchcraft. By possessions possessed. By unnecessary, idiotic wants. To the pitch of mutual savagery and stupor. That's it Father Carlo, I have it now . . . A kind of savage stupor or supineness. On the couch. In front of the television. Have you read about American children, aged five and less? Twenty-seven hours a week in front of the screen.

He gestured towards the calendar on the café wall.

—A billion and a quarter viewers for the *Mundial*. What is your sacramental aspirin compared to television? Compared to the ways in which men's dreams are packaged by advertisement. We make love according to the television images. We masturbate to the cadence of the video-cassette. That is the very genius of capitalism: to package, to put a price-tag on men's dreams. Never to value us beyond our mediocrity. Ladies and gentlemen, the escalator awaits you. We are moving upward together. Towards better sun-tan lotions, towards a faster lawn-mower, to the deep-freeze of your wildest dreams and the stereo and white telephone next to your toilet seat. Hold on: the Holy Grail of cable-pornography for all is in sight. Look: there is the promised land, a Disneyworld for all. And there are gods, Carlo *mio*, in supermarket heaven. Madonna of the sequin tights. And Maradona, he of the hand of God. Has it ever struck you how those two names . . .

He broke off, emptying his drink at a draught. He should not have drunk that second glass. It thrust him forward. He was marooned in his own loquacity, the words thrashing about and spilling.

—The Cold War was no accident. No conspiracy concocted by power-brokers. Communism, perhaps even Stalinism, had horribly overestimated man. As I said . . .

He was repeating himself, he knew. Professorially. He couldn't stop: how accurately America had priced man, reducing him to well-being, making peace between human desires and fulfilment. Stalin starved millions. It's the truth. May he rot for it in hell everlasting. But America made the hungry, the drugged, the ugly invisible. Which is worse? It buttered the souls of men. No matter that the stuff is often margarine, oily, synthetic, golden-yellow. The colour of money. No matter. Fat-free, slimline, daisy-sweet margarine on thirty kinds of bread. Carlo, I'm not making this up, they have thirty different sorts of bread over there: health-breads, croissants, seeded rolls, blueberry muffins, nut-breads, whole wheat, rye, pumpernickle, *panettone* for your dog, for your canary, all spread out in those California emporia.

—How stupid, how cruel it was of those nut-cases, of those prophets in their flea-bitten desert to make man homeless to himself. When there is Los Angeles.

—Bullshit.

Father Carlo said it without rancour.

—Bullshit, *Professore*. The old Party-line blood-libel on human nature and on America. About which, I mean America, you and I really know very little. To me it sounds like the society which says to every man and woman: 'Be what you want to be. Be yourself. This world was not made only for geniuses or neurotics, for the obsessed or the inspired. It was made for you and you and you. If you choose to try and be an artist or a thinker or a pure scholar, that's fine. We will neither inhibit you nor put you on a pedestal. If you prefer to be a couch-potato, an auto-mechanic, a break-dancer, a mile-runner, a broker, if you prefer to be a truck-driver or even a drifter, that's fine too. Perhaps even better. Because it so happens that ideological passion and ascetic illumination, that dogma and sacrifice, have not brought only light and aid to this approximate world of ours. They have sown interminable hatred and self-destruction.' And when America says, 'Just be yourself,' it is not saying, 'Do not better yourself.' It is saying: 'Go after that Nobel Prize if that's what fires your soul. Or that heated swimming-pool.' Not because America believes that heated swimming-pools are the Parthenon or even a necessity. But because they do seem to bring pleasure, and not very much harm. 'Move up the ladder, if you can,' says America, 'because the desire to live decently, to give your family a comfortable home, to send your children to schools better than those you attended yourself, to earn the regard of your neighbours, is not some capitalist vice, but a universal desire.' Do you know, *Professore*, America is just about the first nation and society in human history to encourage common, fallible, frightened humanity to feel at home in its skin.

—Not if that skin is black!

—Even that is coming. Painfully, I know. But inevitably. American democracy . . .

—In which, even at vital elections, only about thirty per cent exercise their right to vote . . .

—But that's the point!

Father Carlo was almost shouting: 'Vote if you will,' says America. 'Our education, our democratic system would have you vote. But if you are too lazy to bother, too ignorant, too bored, well, that's no catastrophe either. There's plenty of history ahead.' It is under the Nazi boot, *Professore*, it is under the

Stalinist truncheon that ninety-nine per cent of all citizens cast their ballots. Do you prefer that to American waywardness?

—I do know this, my dear friend: there are in American affairs black pages, stupidities in plenty. But on balance, America does stand as the one and only great power and community which, unlike any other I know of, is aiming to leave the globe a little better off, a little more hopeful than it finds it. Hope has, in fact, been America's main gross national product and export. Think of Woodrow Wilson, of Roosevelt. Of Lincoln, above all. Ask, if you dare, the millions who have survived under Marxism-Leninism, whether they would rather endure such a regime a day longer, or be penniless immigrants to America or even tenants in an American slum. You know the answer. It is filling the air just now.

—A country which no poem can shake. Where no philosophic argument matters . . .

Father Carlo cut him off.

—I did once hear you declare, at one of those blessed meetings of the Circle, that to exile a man because he differs from points in party orthodoxy is proudly to honour the human spirit. That stupid enormity still drums in my poor head. I have never heard a sane man expound anything more barbaric. If learning, if intellectual argument need to be honoured at that price, if they must feed on intolerance, on condescension, on fatuous authority, to hell with them!

—Like you, *Professore*, I cannot abide rock music. My stomach turns at most television, at the plastic and porn, fast food and illiteracy that pours out of what you call 'California'. But I wonder whether even these things are inflicting on men a fraction of the pain, of the despair which all our Athens, all our high culture have inflicted. They rocked around the clock not long ago to raise millions for charity. They lectured on Kant and played Schubert and went off the same day to stuff millions into gas ovens.

—America may not be for you or me. Not for a communist dreamer and glutton for the printed word. Not for a mendicant friar. But we two are museum exhibits. Incorrigible chatterers. We are ghosts out of the dark of history or pre-history, you said so yourself, *Professore*. Don't you understand? The tidal wave across the Berlin Wall and all the way to Prague and the Pacific is screaming with life. It is the insurrection of the young, even when they are eighty years old. Your dogma, your tyranny of the ideal, pumped youth out of human lives. Under despotism children are born old. Just look at the eyes and mouths in those pictures from Romania. And if America is childish, as it may be, what a lucky failing that is! Fountain of Youth? What he found may be Coca-Cola. But it does bubble!

—It rots your teeth. You Jesuit. You casuistical Jesuit.

They were walking again, briskly and aimlessly, towards the southbound boulevard and the war memorial.

—We are, Father Carlo, a murderous, greedy, unclean species. But we have produced Plato and Schubert, to use your own examples, Shakespeare and Einstein. It follows that there are differences in worth between human endeavours. *Credo*: that it is intrinsically finer for a human being to be obsessed by an algebraic problem, a Mozart canon or a Cézanne composition than by the manufacture of automobiles or the trading of shares. That a teacher, a scholar, a thinker, even, God have mercy, a priest is almost immeasurably more valuable and nearer the dignity of hope than is a prize-fighter, a broker, a soap powder magnate. *Credo* again: that the mystery of creative and analytic genius is just that, a mystery, and that it is given to the very few. But that lesser beings can be woken to its presence and exposed to its demands. Oh I know, on a free vote it is the bingo hall and the dog-track that will prevail, not the theatre of Aeschylus. I know that hundreds of millions of our fellow men prefer football to chamber music and would rather become glazed in front of a soap opera or blue movie than pick up a book, let alone a serious book. Amen to all that, says capitalism. Let their choice be free. Let them stew in their well-being. Hippos are free to wallow in their mud. Why not man? But that, Carlo—

And once more they stood on the pavement facing each other.

—is to hold man in utter contempt. It is to turn history into a graveyard for used cars. Marxism tried otherwise. It filled the symphony halls and the libraries. It gave teachers and writers a living wage. What matters more, it gave them an eminent status in society; it made museums free of charge, open to all. It taught that a great theorem or sonata or philosophic principle comes nearer the bone of man, of our nascent humanity, than does the latest hit on a pop chart.

The sounds in the air, even their own resumed motion, appeared to get busier with the imminence of daybreak.

—I agree with you, *Professore*. I wouldn't be feeling the wet pavement through my shoes if I didn't. I agree with every word, my dear orator. But I cannot see by what authority, by what right, you or I can cram *our* values—yes, they are mine too—down other men's throats. You claim to be arguing from love for the common man, from what you call an overestimate of his means. But that love is filled with contempt and oppression. The pursuit of quality, your blueprint for excellence, comes with the lash. The price is too high. We have seen that.

—Hypocrisy, Father Carlo, hypocrisy and cant! If you honestly believed that, how could you be a priest, even half of one? How could you be a teacher, imparting knowledge to others, forcing it, as you put it, down their often unwilling throats? Every little step forward is made of sweat and mutiny. Until the insight is won, until the craft is mastered. No one has ever learned or achieved anything worth having without being stretched beyond themselves, till their bones crack. 'Easy does it,' says America to mankind. But easy has never done it. Never. I don't want to know how long it takes to produce a bottle of Coca-Cola or an instant hamburger or a tranquillizer. I do know that it takes six hundred years for the grapes to become what they are in those hills around us, six hundred years of back-breaking toil and silent cunning. Years in which hail almost flattens them or in which the heat is too fierce or during which they have been ploughed under.

—Why, then, did you define socialism as impatience?

—I don't know.

As if at the edge of the pavement, in a stillness.

—Of late, I do get things muddled, Carlo. A slow impatience. Something like that.

And abruptly, he seized his companion's elbow: I am a

socialist. I am and remain a Marxist. Because otherwise I could not be a proof-reader!

The self-evidence of it burst on him. He wanted to fling his arms wide, to dance on that very spot.

—If California triumphs, there will be no need of proof-readers. Machines will do it better. Or all texts will be audio-visual, with self-correctors built in. Night after night after night, Carlo, I work till my brain aches. So as to get it absolutely right. So as to correct the minutest misprint in a text which no one may ever read or which will be shredded the next day. Getting it right. The holiness of it. The self-respect. *Gran Dio*, Carlo, you must see what I'm driving at. Utopia simply means *getting it right*! Communism means taking the *errata* out of history. Out of man. Reading proofs.

He was out of breath. What a queer picture they must make, Carlo pacing, he on his toes, under the first distant volley of bells. Matins and the wail of a siren from the river.

—I can't match all your clever arguments, *mio* Carlo. You may even be right about America. And I know what they would have done to an outsider like myself—am I some sort of Leninist Albigensian?—over there, in the east. But I believe in my belief. What else is there for me now?

More bells, out of unison, querulous and booming. An early bus drove past, and he saw the tow-headed driver yawning hugely. A metal shutter was cranked up, and electric light from a kiosk spilled down the road. Sunday morning sounds thickened at every moment. A bus in the opposite direction, just out of the depot.

Carlo said: Look at that sky-light over there. Under the chimney-pots. Just over there. Morning.

He followed the pointing finger. To see better, he closed one eye.

9

—Open both eyes, if you please. Wide. Hold steady.

The ophthalmologist's buttery breath enveloped him.

—Keep open. Try not to blink.

The drops had dilated his pupils. Now the harness through which the eye doctor was peering held his chin rigid and pressed on his forehead.

—You can close for a moment.

Darkness and a vague impression of swimming.

—Open again. Now look up. Down. To the left. Left again. Hold. Now to the right.

The man's voice was absurdly close, but coming at him as through a rubber tunnel.

—You can relax now.

The apparatus glided away. Dr Melchiori switched on the overhead light and returned to his roll-top desk. He scribbled. There was a stain on the back of his white coat. It must have been sizeable if he could make it out, for the room was blurred and the letters on the wall-chart quivered and merged.

—It will take a while for the drops to wear off. Be careful when you leave. There are steps. And they're digging up the road. As usual.

He continued making furious notes and flipped once more through the cards on which he had inscribed the measurements taken during the examination.

—I shall prescribe medication. An ointment and drops. To ease the strain. Three times daily. Make sure the drops reach the cornea and the corners of the eye.

For a moment it sounded like a dismissal and the end of a routine visit. Then the doctor motioned to him to come nearer, to sit not on the narrow metal stool next to the instruments but in the chair by the desk.

—You're not a child. So I had best be frank with you.

The doctor scrutinized his notes and seemed vexed: Profession: proof-reader, text-editor. A trade, my dear sir, not exactly calculated to make things easy for your eyes. How long have you been at it?

The doctor glanced at his records and nodded.

—More than thirty-five years. As I thought. Why, in heaven's name, did you not come to me before? Why?

He spun on his chair, aggrieved.

—You say that the morning discomforts, what you call 'a burning behind the eyes,' began only a few months ago. But why waste even those months? I know: we have waiting lists. The service is overrun. You'll often find me at this desk fifteen or sixteen hours at a stretch. I do realize . . . but in emergencies! When the case is acute. As yours is. I can't hide that from you. I don't hold with baby-talk. Melchiori tells his patients the facts. In plain language.

—There are no miracles. The weakness in the left eye must go back a very long way. Possibly congenital. You did say that your mother wore glasses, didn't you? And you have, my friend, been favouring the right eye far longer, far more intensely than you realize. There was going to be a problem whatever you did. But with your job and this regrettable delay . . .

Bruno Melchiori looked at him, seeking, soliciting approbation, fiddling with the switch at the base of the desk-lamp. Then he turned back to his notes. Exasperated, commiserative.

—The fact is that there is in your left eye little but peripheral vision and that the strain on the right has already caused considerable damage. Considerable. There is a small tear in the retina, just here.

He thrust a rough sketch across the desk.

—Had you come to me in good time, it would have been worth operating on the left eye. To remove those cataracts. To implant a lens. As matters stand now . . .

His voice seeped away.

—You are, of course, most welcome to seek a second opinion. Perhaps you should insist on having one. In my judgement, an operation would bring only discomfort and false hopes. The left eye is going on strike, dear sir, on permanent strike. So our real problem is the right.

The doctor half turned away, and as to himself: Can you change your employment? I didn't think so. What I can do is to give you a medical authorization for a few weeks of leave. The right eye *must* rest. It is infected and must have complete rest. Otherwise . . . You do understand me? If you don't give it a rest . . .

The ancient gesture of doleful impotence, palms upward.

—As is, I cannot be too optimistic. Plain words are what I

believe in. Your sight will diminish significantly. Whether or not we decide to operate. Whether or not surgery succeeds. The problem with glaucoma and related conditions . . . But I won't bore or alarm you with technicalities. As do so many of my esteemed colleagues.

Melchiori's chin quivered.

—With rest and regular treatment much can be salvaged. But to leave things so late . . .

The nurse, in the swarming corridor of the clinic, helped him impatiently into his coat. When he reached the street, which swam before him in a half-light, he ransacked his pockets for the prescription. But he could not help noticing that the rasp of the tram-car brakes had taken on a new sharpness.

10

They gave him a fortnight's leave and tinted glasses. Time turned grey. As if a drowsy wasp were droning and knitting the hours.

He had resolved on method. A touch of physical exercise in the morning (a man's toes, as he bends towards them, can induce melancholy). Three solid hebdomadal sessions at the municipal library, where he would re-read, so as to renew the armoury of his soul, Marx's *Eighteenth Brumaire*—how he remembered the trumpet shock of his first brush with that text—and the incandescent jeremiads of Trotsky on Stalin. But he had been told not to read very much and to give his veiled eyes a furlough. Moreover, there were the newspapers, fanned out on a table at the entrance to the reading room. With their fat headlines and arresting pictures. The vacuous shelves and bread-lines in Russian cities. The indictment of Party officials in East Germany and Bulgaria. Royalists unfurling banners in Romania. Gorbachev pirouetting for loans and hand-outs in what had been, not long ago, the Escorial of Franco. He read. He thrust the captions close to his right eye as if the Medusa held him fast in her stony smile. And then he sat at the library table, incapable of serious attention.

The winter park was no better. The thinning pigeons seemed to glare at him as if he were a rival for breadcrumbs and peanut shells. The statue of and to Garibaldi, turbaned, his curved blade operatic, with its chiselled promise of emancipation for the common man, struck him as insufferable. He played games with its lapidary syllables, substituting vowels, inverting letters. The resulting obscenities were out of an adolescent's lavatory. A passing couple, tourists, guidebook in hand and muffled against the raw wind, asked him, in halting courtesy, for directions to the Museum of the Resistance. Promptly, loquaciously, he misdirected them. Realizing, as they thankfully departed, that they were Jews, most probably Israelis on some visitation of remembrance. A numbing distaste flooded through him. Against himself, but also against the innocent. As if it was indeed the stiff dolour of the Jews, their inability to let be, which had brought the political and ideological world to its present chaos.

When he told Maura, elaborating the incident in self-reproach, she flinched. Not only then. His constricted emptiness grated on her. She was, just at this time, fiercely overworked and, he sensed, self-sufficient.

Almost involuntarily, he drifted back to the print-works. Away from the barrens of his supposed rest. His temporary replacement—but was he only that?—tolerated his presence on a cast-off stool in a corner of the eyrie. Let him sit there while he, the young man with the keen glance, scanned the wet pages. The floor quivered to the mallet-strokes of the rotors. One night, the new man vanished to the toilets (a complaisance he had virtually sought to deny himself when total concentration was of the essence). Compulsively, he lifted from the desk one of the sheets, corrected, already initialled and ready to go. He spotted, at once, as if through antennae in his skin, as if with second or third sight exact beyond any in his failing retina, two errors: an accent out of place and a letter in a wrong font. He reached for the red biro.

—For Christ's sake, breathed the young copy-editor who had returned behind him, cat-like up the metal steps.

—For Christ's sake.

Not in outright annoyance, but softly, with a hint of derision.

—Nothing escapes the Owl, does it? I've heard all about you. Holding up urgent jobs for a second or third look. The perfectionist.

He plucked the offending page and laughed outright.

—Do you know what this is? Have you bothered to look? Or don't you read but only proof-read? Have a closer look, maestro.

He thrust the print at him.

—This is a handbill. For an auction of used farm implements and manure sacks! To be held in the co-operative of San Maurizio—God knows where that hole is—on Tuesday next. One hundred copies. To be stuck on some outhouse door or dumped in the next ditch. And you worry about an accent!

—Desperately. Do you know what the cabala teaches? That the sum total of the evil and miseries of humankind arose when a lazy or incompetent scribe misheard, took down erroneously, a single letter, one single solitary letter, in Holy Writ. Every horror since has come on us through and because of that one *erratum*. You didn't know that, did you?

They faced off in the thumping obscurity and stood speechless as the runner-boy stopped by and scooped up the pile of corrected, imperfect bills.

—You're no help, you know. They haven't dared tell you. The schedules are being tightened. Your sort of practice may suit printers of fine books and copper-plate work. But not here.

The next packet had just landed on his raked table.

—Not here.

—On the contrary. It is just here that it matters more than ever before. To act otherwise is utter contempt. Contempt for those who cannot afford to look at a fine book, at quality paper or crafted type. Contempt for those who have a right under God, yes under God, to have a flawless handbill, also for a sale of manure! It is just for those who live in rural holes, in slums, that we should do the best work. So that some spark of perfection will enter their wretched days. Can't you understand, how much contempt there is in a false accent or a misplaced serif? As if you spat at another human being.

His understudy stared at him. Neutrally. As from some later planet.

—You can sit over there if you want. But let me get on with it.

And towards the dead hour of first dawn: Let me get you some coffee, rabbi.

He started at the epithet. He watched embarrassed as his sharer drew back to himself a sheet already initialled and read it a second time.

11

He had taken the trip on an impulse. Probably ill-considered. Even the special excursion fare to Rome intended, he wryly noted, for pilgrims in quest of remission and absolution at the holy places, sapped his budget—one now stretched to the limit because he knew he would only be able to resume his proof-reading part-time, if at all. It was a loan from Tullio which had made possible his overnight stay in a grotty *pensione* near the railway station. Dutiful but hurried hands had assisted him down the steep steps from the carriage to the platform. He was on his own in the blaring rush of the city. As a child, he had rubbed his eyeballs to provoke crystalline star-showers. Cleaning his glasses obsessively, blinking hard, all he could produce now was an undulant mist.

He knew Rome's orange grey and the fumed light which gave to many of its monumentalities their ghostly weight. On a much earlier visit, he had been made uneasy by the mottled air and the sepia wash which lay, day in and day out, on the august walls and arches. But this time the dun veil, which floated between himself and the illustrious sites, hung within. He walked slowly, hesitated at corners and picked at railings.

The nastiness had been reported, very briefly, at the bottom of a column of miscellaneous crimes in the national press. The plaque in the street of the Narrow Shops in Rome had been vandalized by unknown, though presumably neo-fascist or royalist defacers.

He remembered how he had found that plaque, years ago, and how he had deposited, at the foot of the wall, a small bunch of violets. The event commemorated was one among hundreds no less atrocious enacted on those antique streets and squares between 1943 and liberation. Fifteen members of a communist underground resistance group had been betrayed into the hands of the *Waffen* SS by an elderly, observant housekeeper prone to insomnia. They had been tortured. So far as could be discovered, not one had broken and given up further names. Not the sixteen-year-old boy whose testicles they had put in a carpenter's vice. Not the three young women whose bodies had been chequered with cigarette burns. Not the old man (the name suggested that he was a Jew) whose beard they had torn out hair by hair and whose hands they inserted in a door-jamb. They then had dragged their prisoners to the narrow street, propped them against the wall and machine-gunned them. One of the victims, his legs smashed during interrogation, had slipped to his knees when the SS opened fire. Seeing him alive, they kicked him to death, slowly. For years, it was said, the runnels and star-splashes of human blood could be made out like fading burns on the stone.

Standing in front of the inscription on his visit long ago, testing its lettering and the incision of the Party badge, he had, almost unawares, committed to memory a number of the names. Bartani (Adriana). Pradone (Vigilio)—the boy. Gilodi (Manuele). Together with their dates of birth. Comrades. Rostagni (Marco), aged twenty-three when they strapped him to the table. Condini (Fabio), the leader of the cell who had, on the very eve of the war, published in a clandestine edition that notable essay on Marx's reading of Lucretius. Comrades in arms about whose courage and sacrifice there could be no question and whose doomed faith and actions had cleansed Rome of some part of its unholiness, of its self-betrayals.

Encasing these names in his memory, adverting to them on occasion, he imagined he was practising something like the Jewish rite of *kaddish*. The refusal to forget, to let death have the final say over lives which must remain living.

He was not alone. A small group had gathered in the

Botteghe Oscure. The memorial had not only been smeared with the double-lightning of the SS across a Star of David ludicrously misshapen, but part of the marble had also been chipped away, and a rough fissure now sliced through the column of names. Those assembled, they amounted to perhaps a dozen, stared at the damage. One or two had brought fresh flowers. These lay at the rim of the gutter amid the chippings of rent stone and the dribble of brown paint. The right brown, he noted, that of the shirts.

A very old man was shaking helplessly, his sobs out of control. He managed the name of Santori (Anna Maria).

—She was my sister. My sister. They raped her first. She kept saying 'Stalingrad'. So they tore out her teeth. Anna Maria. I am Guiseppe Santori.

He turned to the bystanders for confirmation.

A tall man in a sheepskin jacket, the collar raised, said: Bastards. Fascist bastards. And walked off abruptly.

It was the woman just in front of him, long motionless, who turned and spoke to him.

—Now they are going to change the name of the Party. I call that spitting on the dead. Doing dirt on them greater than this. We expect this sort of shit from the fascist swine. But now it is the Party—forgive my language—pissing on history.

She had steeled herself to say the word aloud and carried on more freely.

—My mother was one of them. She happened to be away carrying messages to the partisans in Orvieto when the SS came. Otherwise . . .

She looked at the stained names.

—She knew who betrayed them. The foul bitch died only a few years ago. In a cosy home for the aged. Paid for by your and my taxes, *Signor*.

The laugh was forced.

—My mother unearthed her not long after the Americans came. She wanted to have her arrested and put away. I imagine she was even ready to kill her. But the hag cringed and whined and offered Mother bits of hideous jewellery and money. Mother vomited and left her blubbering on the floor. But the Party is no better. It is betraying them all over again. I can wager that they would rather not replace the plaque. So embarrassing. Men and women done to death with the names of Togliatti, of Stalin, yes of Stalin, in their hearts.

She shut her lips tight and turned away. He saw the slow shiver of anger and disgust pass through her shoulders. Now her back trembled. His hand was on her arm. She did not remove it but drew it more closely to her when she saw him fumbling at the edge of the steps which led to the *piazza*. She was, he decided, beautiful.

In the diminutive *trattoria* confidence flowed easily. They had agreed to share the bill, but the thin wine, he insisted, was to be on his side of the ledger. She sold plastic and fake leather bags, belts, gloves, accessories and costume bangles in a boutique behind Via Veneto. At first, she kept eyeing her watch. Then, with shy bravado and over a second cup of coffee, she announced that she was taking the afternoon off. Let them dock her wretched pay if they chose. She detested the job anyway; the odour of celluloid and varnish, the customers pawing the goods endlessly and then complaining about their own finger-marks on the fabric.

Yes, she would take today off. In homage to the defiled dead. How her mother had feared and scorned shopkeepers, she who had been an educated woman but tubercular.

Her own existence? Quickly inventoried. A father who escaped, as into air, soon after her birth. Trade-school. The years as receptionist in a garage and repair-yard on the road to Ostia. Oh, indeed, quite close to the one in which Pasolini had been knifed. Then, a shadow in her left lung. A less taxing employment, or so it sounded, in diverse emporia and boutiques.

No, it had not worked out. The man was of some intelligence and political decency, but restless. They had parted more or less amicably. The first few postcards had come from Tunis. Then nothing. Yes (and she was at ease reporting it), there had been episodes since. But something in the incompletion of her ways—the phrase intrigued him—seemed to exclude others. Or it might be, and her smile quickened the light all around her, that those who came too near to her, to these incompletions and jagged edges, felt—how should she put it?—superfluous or scratched. At this image she reddened and laughed into her wine.

But what of him?

When they got up, the *trattoria* had emptied, and the waiter was wiping neighbouring tables with palpable reproof.

Nothing like it had ever happened to him before.

With its unspoken self-evidence.

He did not recall their progress through immaterial streets, only the firm tug of her arm as she conducted him across loud tram-rails, around ruts and steep pavements. Nor did he really remember their ascent in the clanging lift. What was vivid to his recollection was her low warm laugh as she fumbled at her key-ring and failed, twice, to use the right key to open her own door. They undressed each other like children in a lost game. Her lips sped across his whole body and lingered where it was worn. The loveliness of her arched back pierced him with wonder. His fingers idled in her unpinned hair as she knelt. When he entered her and let that high soundless wave carry him, a single word sounded in his unbound being: 'dormition'. He had read it in a catalogue of old masters and did not know quite what it meant. Not so he could define it. But in that motion towards and with her, dormition seemed to signify a waking sleep, a peace and rest so whole as to be on the other side, on the lit and southern side of sleep.

In the darkening afternoon they spoke of this and that. In abbreviated yet long-familiar phrases. It was only when putting on his clothes that he noticed the stack of cuttings and pamphlets on her dresser. Horoscopes, astrological charts, predictions of planetary conjunctions to come and of their portent. She beamed at him full of confident zeal.

What, exactly, were the hour and the day of his nativity? She would read his palm for that also was a science of which she had some knowledge. The desecration they had witnessed that morning and which had brought them together, Taurus and Libra, had been foretold. That is why she had turned to him so naturally. No less forseeable was the return of the Communist Party to repute and power. When Jupiter and enigmatic Neptune were in the house of the Lion. There could be no shadow of doubt. Not for those who would see. Once baleful Saturn had moved out of Scorpio . . .

She reached for a tract and pressed it on him. What had been his mother's astral sign, her favourite precious stone?

—Tell me, please.

They parted strangers, and he hurried to the station.

12

He was walking too fast. Twice already, he had come up hard against edges and breaks in the pavement. Now his feet caught in a discarded carrier-bag, its garish design malignantly alive in the wind. He kicked blindly at the thing.

A sentence sprayed on the back of the bus-stop shelter seized his notice. 'God does not believe in God.'

To which a lesser hand, armed only with red chalk, had added the word *our*: 'God does not believe in our God.'

Absurdly, a touch of fear stung him, and the momentary, deranged conviction that a deserted universe, like a house unlocked after the removal vans had gone, would sink into oblivion if he failed to carry out his present purpose. He felt the inane certitude that this enactment, so trivial in itself, was the litany of which Father Carlo had once told him, whose recitation, out of however gutted and reduced a human mouth and soul, kept reality going and coerced the tired future into its advent.

Shivering in the cold, he wiped his glasses and pressed on.

Though he knew his city well, the building was not easy to find. Instead of the customary name-plate by the entrance, he was able to make out only a bent card, illegibly inscribed, and pinned to the downstairs letter-box. The stairs lay in thick shadow and he groped uselessly for the light-switch. At the fifth landing, he found the door closed. He pulled at the bell. The sound came back muffled and distant. He pulled again and waited. He was about to reverse his steps when the door inched open. He could not really see the figure behind the crack.

What was it he wanted?

He stated his intent.

If anything, the opening narrowed even more.

Was he a practical joker? A provocateur?

Urgently he leaned against the door handle.

—Nothing of the kind!

He advanced his name, the date of his original adherence, the number on his Party card. He inventoried his Party assignments and activities.

Was he babbling? The sad notion crossed his mind.

He cited the names of several Comrades who could vouch for him, who knew of his purposed recantation.

A muted, theatrical laugh on the other side of the door. But the opening widened.

Innerly, to be perfectly honest, he had never left the Party. He had only sought to clear up for himself, at a time of especial internal contradictions, certain theoretical conundra (it was too late to rescind that pretentious, evasive word). Certain perplexities which had also troubled other comrades. He had been wrong. He knew that now. As Bukharin had taught: deviants, however right *subjectively*, belong to the limbo of history.

Again the miserly laugh. But the door opened.

The man was in slippers and a smell of fish clung to his sweater. A pan—soup, coffee?—was spluttering behind a curtained recess. Parallel to the door, as in a second line of defence, stood a table. Printed forms, roneoed sheets, cigarette ash. Now he saw that the man held an unlit cigarette between his lips.

—You *are* a queer one, aren't you, *Professore*. Isn't that what they called you? Always talking. Talk, talk. If you ask me, that's where we made our big mistake. There's no pay-off in talk. Take to the streets. Smash their fucking skulls. Occupy the factories. That's what I always said.

The surly recognition, the recall of his mocking sobriquet, filled him with rare joy. He was eager to debate the issue, to identify the leftist infantilism (Lenin's decisive tag) of the man's position. But checked himself and asked with humility whether he could apply for reinstatement.

—Haven't you heard?

The man motioned towards a scatter of cards half-hidden under a file at one end of the table.

—Those are just this past week's. Most tear up their Party cards or stuff them in the incinerator. But some do send theirs. With obscenities attached. Shall I read them to you, comrade?

That would not be necessary, and he heard the irony in the mode of address. Yet he flushed with contentment.

—By next month, honoured sir, there may not be a Party.

Ah, but there would be, leaner, more astringent, better armed theoretically. The truth knows no circumstance. Tullio was wrong. If God no longer believed in God, the time had come for man to believe in man. Only Marxism could make that belief effective.

The man cut him off with a shrug. He drew a creased form from one of the piles and nudged it across the table. An application for membership. He would pass it on to the committee. Which had not, in weeks, succeeded in assembling a quorum. There was a small fee for processing.

He had the notes ready. The man counted them and considered him with distaste.

—The Party will examine your case. And that's what you must be, believe me. A case.

The lame play on words seemed to trigger silent mirth. He shook his head.

—You'll hear from us.

Then he looked down at the form which the applicant had begun to fill in.

—Don't you even read a paper? Haven't you heard? 'I hereby apply for acceptance in the Communist Party.' There is no such thing, my friend! There is no more PCI. *Basta. Finito.*

Detaching each funereal syllable, he slid the flat of his hand across his windpipe.

—Gone and buried, the old whore. It is now the Party of the Democratic Left.

He spelled out the new initials hoarsely.

—No more red star. A green tree. Look here: a bushy green tree.

He waved the new logo in front of the *Professore*'s face.

—Is that what you want to join? Well, is it?

It was. So precisely that the penitent could find no rejoinder, no words for his thirst. Only a puppet's quick unseeing nod.

The man cleared his throat impatiently, spat into a grey handkerchief and bade him write his address. In capital letters, if you please.

He would be receiving a summons from the district committee.

—Though only God knows when.

God did seem much about in the city these days. So be it. The real battle lay ahead.

The door shut loudly.

It was only at the bottom of the stair-well, still in pitch blackness, that he realized he had not held on to the banister. Not even once. But then one doesn't need to, does one, when coming home.

GRANTA

Martin Amis

Time's Arrow

I, Odilo Unverdorben, arrived in Auschwitz Central somewhat precipitately and by motorbike, with a wide twirl or frill of slush and mud, shortly after the Bolsheviks had entrained their ignoble withdrawal. *Now*. Was there a secret passenger on the back seat of the bike, or in some imaginary sidecar? No. I was one. I was also in full uniform. Beyond the southern boundary of the Lager, in a roofless barn, I slipped out of our coarse travelling clothes and emotionally donned the black boots, the white coat, the fleece-lined jacket, the peaked cap, the pistol. The motorbike I found earlier, wedged into a ditch. Oh how I soared out of there, with what vaulting eagerness, what daring . . . Now I straddled this heavy machine and revved with jerked gauntlet. Auschwitz lay around me, miles and miles of it, like a somersaulted Vatican. Human life was all ripped and torn. But I was one now, fused for a preternatural purpose.

Your shoulder-blades still jolted to the artillery of the Russians as they scurried eastward. What had they done here? Done something as an animal does: just finds it's gone ahead and done it. I reacted on impulse. To tell the truth, I was in less than perfect control of myself. I started shouting (they sounded like shouts of pain and rage). And at whom? At these coat-hangers and violin bows, at these aitches and queries and crawling double-U's, ranked like tabloid expletives? I marched; I marched, shouting, over the bridge and across all the railway tracks and into the birch wood—into the place I would come to know as Birkenau. After a short and furious rest in the potato store I entered the women's hospital, inflexibly determined on an

---

The narrator exists inside the body of a man who is living his life backwards in time. He first appears as a senior citizen in the American northeast, where he works in a suburban health centre. Later, under another name, he works for many years in a city hospital in New York. He sails for Europe in 1948; he lives quietly for a while, under another name, in Portugal; when the war begins, in 1945, he goes to Rome and visits the Vatican, where he establishes his final identity; he then travels north towards Poland. *M.A.*

inspection. It was not appropriate. I see that now (it was a swoon of where-to-begin?). My arrival only deepened the stupefaction of the few orderlies, never mind the patients, sprawled two or three to a straw sack and still well short of the size of a woman. And rats as big as cats! I was astonished by the power with which my German crashed out of me, as if in millennial anger at having been silenced for so long. In the washroom another deracinating spectacle: marks and pfennigs—good tender—stuck to the wall with human ordure. A mistake: a mistake. What is the *meaning* of this? Ordure, ordure everywhere. Even on my return through the ward, past ulcer and edema, past sleepwalker and sleeptalker, I could feel the hungry suck of it on the soles of my black boots. Outside: everywhere. This stuff, this human stuff, at normal times (and in civilized locales) tastefully confined to the tubes and runnels, subterranean, unseen—this stuff had burst its banks, surging outward and upward on to the floor, the walls, the very ceiling of life. Naturally, I didn't immediately see the logic and justice of it. I didn't immediately see this: that now human shit is out in the open, we'll get a chance to find out what this stuff can really do.

That first morning I was served a rudimentary breakfast in the Officers' Home. I felt quite calm, though I could neither eat nor drink. With my ham and cheese, which were not of my making, they brought me iced seltzer. There was only one other officer present. I was keen to exercise my German, but we didn't speak. He held his coffee cup as a woman does, with both palms curled around it, for the warmth; and you could hear the china tapping its morse against his teeth. On several occasions he stood up with some serenity and went to the bathroom, and dived back in again gracelessly scrabbling at his belt. This, I soon saw, was a kind of acclimatization. For the first few weeks I was seldom off the toilet bowl myself.

My utterly silent cubicle has a shallow orange bathmat on the floor beside the bed. To welcome the faint dampness of my German feet, as I turn in. To welcome the faint dampness of my German feet, as I rise.

During week two the camp started filling up. In dribs and drabs, at first, then in flocks and herds. All this I watched through a spyhole, under a workbench in a disused supply hut towards the birch wood, with blanket, kümmel bottle—and rosary, fingered like an abacus, as I counted them in. I realized I had seen a few of these same processions on my way north through eastern Czechoslovakia, in Gottwaldor and in Ostrava. The hearty trek and the bracing temperatures had obviously done the men good, though their condition, on arrival, still left much to be desired. And *there weren't enough of them.* As in a dream one was harrowed by questions of scale, by impenetrable disparities. In their hundreds, even in their thousands, these stragglers could never fill the gaping universe of the Kat-Zet. Another source, another powerhouse, was desperately needed . . . The short days were half over by the time I ventured from the hut (where my motorbike was also preserved. I kept examining it in a fond fever). The officers' clubroom was busier now, and there were always new arrivals. It felt strange—no, it felt right that we should all know each other, as it were automatically: we, who had gathered here for a preternatural purpose. My German worked like a dream, like a brilliant robot you switch on and stand back and admire as it does all the hard work. Courage was arriving too, in uniformed human units, the numbers and the special daring adequate to the task we faced. How handsome men are. I mean their shoulders, their tremendous necks. By the end of the second week our clubhouse was the scene of strident song and bold laughter. One night, bumping into the doorway, and stepping over a somnolent colleague, I made my way out into the sleet, the toilets all being occupied, and as I crouched, steadying my cheeks against the cold planks, I peered through the reeking shadows of Auschwitz and saw that the nearest ruins were fuming more than ever and had even begun to glow. There was a new smell in the air. The sweet smell.

We needed magic, to resolve significance from what surrounded us, which scarcely permitted contemplation: we needed someone godlike—someone who could turn this world around. And in due course he came . . . Not a tall man, but of the usual dimensions; coldly beautiful, true, with self-delighted eyes; graceful, chasteningly graceful in his athletic authority; and a doctor. Yes, a simple doctor. It was quite an entrance, I don't mind telling you. Flashing through the birch wood came the white Mercedes-Benz, from which he leapt in his greatcoat and then dashed across the yard yelling out orders. I knew his name, and murmured it as I looked on from the supply hut, with my schnapps and my toilet paper: 'Uncle Pepi'. The trash and wreckage before him was now shivering with fire as he stood, hands on hips, watching all his powers gather in the smoke. I turned slowly away and felt the rush and zip of violently animated matter. When, with a shout, I jerked my eye back to its hole there was no smoke anywhere, only the necessary building, perfect, even to the irises and the low picket fence that lined its path, before which 'Uncle Pepi' now stood, with one arm crooked and raised. Even to the large sign above the door: BRAUSEBAD. 'Sprinkleroom', I whispered, with a reverent snort. But now 'Uncle Pepi' moved on. That morning, as I lay with my teeth chattering in anticipation on the wooden floor of the supply hut, I heard five more explosions. Velocity and fusion sucking up the shocked air. By the next day we were ready to go to work.

What tells me that this is right? What tells me that all the rest was wrong? Certainly not my aesthetic sense. I would never claim that Auschwitz-Birkenau-Monowitz was good to look at. Or to listen to, or to smell, or to taste, or to touch. There was, among my colleagues there, a general though desultory quest for greater elegance. I can understand that word, and all its yearning: *elegant*. Not for its elegance did I come to love the evening sky, hellish red with the gathering souls. Creation is easy. Also ugly. *Hier ist kein warum.* Here there is no why. Here there is no when, no how, no where. Our preternatural purpose? To dream a race. To make a people from the weather. From thunder and from lightning. With gas, with electricity, with shit, with fire.

I or a doctor of equivalent rank was present at every stage in the sequence. One did not need to know why the ovens were so ugly, so very ugly. A tragically burly insect eight feet tall and made out of rust. Who would want to cook with an oven such as this? Pulleys, plungers, grates and vents were the organs of the machine . . . The patients, still dead, were delivered out on a stretcher-like apparatus. The air felt thick and warped with the magnetic heat of creation. Thence to the Chamber, where the bodies were stacked carefully and, in my view, counter-intuitively, with babies and children at the base of the pile, then the women and the elderly, and then the men. It was my stubborn belief that it would be better the other way round, because the little ones surely risked injury under that press of naked weight. But it worked. Sometimes, my face rippling peculiarly with smiles and frowns, I would monitor proceedings through the viewing slit. There was usually a long wait while the gas was invisibly introduced by the ventilation grilles. Dead bodies have their dead body language. It says nothing. The dead look so dead. I always felt a gorgeous relief at the moment of the first stirring. Then it was ugly again. Well, we cry and twist and are naked at both ends of life. We cry at both ends of life, while the doctor watches. It was I, Odilo Unverdorben, who personally removed the pellets of Zyklon B and entrusted them to the pharmacist in his white coat. Next, the façade of the Sprinkleroom, the function of whose spouts and nozzles (and numbered seats and wardrobe tickets, and signs in six or seven languages) was merely to reassure and not, alas, to cleanse; and the garden path beyond.

Clothes, spectacles, hair, spinal braces and so on—these came later. Entirely intelligibly, though, to prevent needless suffering, the dental work was usually completed while the patients were not yet alive. The *kapos* would go at it, crudely but effectively, with knives or chisels or any tool that came to hand. Most of the gold we used, of course, came direct from the *Reichsbank*. But every German present, even the humblest, gave willingly of his own store—I more than any other officer save 'Uncle Pepi' himself. I *knew* my gold had a sacred efficacy. All those years I amassed it, and polished it with my mind: for the Jews' teeth. The bulk of the clothes was contributed by the Reich Youth Leadership. Hair for the Jews came courtesy of Filzfabrik A. G. of Roth, near Nuremburg. Freightcars full of it. Freightcar after freightcar.

At this point, notwithstanding, I should like to log one of several possible caveats or reservations. In the Sprinkleroom the patients eventually get dressed in the clothes provided, which, though seldom very clean, are at least always pertinently cut. Here, the guards have a habit of touching the women. Sometimes —certainly—to bestow a jewel, a ring, a small valuable. But at other times quite gratuitously. Oh, I think they mean well enough. It is done in the irrepressible German manner: coltishly, and with lit face. And they only do it to the angry ones. And it definitely has the effect of calming them down. One touch, there, and they go all numb and blocked, like the others. (Who wail sometimes. Who stare at us with incredulous scorn. But I understand their condition. I'm sympathetic; I accept all that.) It may be symbolic, this touching of the women. Life and love must go on. Life and love must emphatically and resonantly go on: here, that's what we're all about. Yet there is a patina of cruelty, intense cruelty, as if creation corrupts . . . I don't want to touch the girls' bodies. As is well known, I frown on such harassment. I don't even want to look at them. The bald girls with their enormous eyes. Just made, and all raw from their genesis. I'm a *little* worried by it: I mean, this fastidiousness is so out of character. The delicacy of the situation, with their parents and often their grandparents there and everything (as in a thwarted erotic dream), would hardly explain the lack of visual stimulation; and I get on like a house on fire with the girls in the officers' bordello. No. I think it must have something to do with my wife.

The overwhelming majority of the women, the children and the elderly we process with gas and fire. The men, of course, as is right, walk a different path to recovery. *Arbeit Macht Frei* says the sign on the gate, with typically gruff and undesigning eloquence. The men work for their freedom. There they go now, in the autumn dusk, the male patients in their light pajamas, while the band plays. They march in ranks of five, in their wooden clogs. Look. There's a thing they do, with their heads. They bend their heads right back until their faces are entirely open to the sky. I've tried it. I try to do it, and I can't.

There's this fist of flesh at the base of my neck, which the men don't yet have. The men come here awful thin. You can't get a stethoscope to them. The bell bridges on their ribs. Their hearts sound far away.

There they go, to the day's work, with their heads bent back. I was puzzled at first but now I know why they do it, why they stretch their throats like that. They are looking for the souls of their mothers and their fathers, their women and their children, gathering in the heavens—awaiting human form, and union . . . The sky above the Vistula is full of stars. I can see them now. They no longer hurt my eyes.

These familial unions and arranged marriages, known as *selections on the ramp*, were the regular highpoints of the Kat-Zet routine. It is a commonplace to say that the triumph of Auschwitz was essentially organizational: we found the sacred fire that hides in the human heart—and built an autobahn that went there. But how to explain the divine synchronies of the ramp? At the very moment that the weak and young and old were brought from the Sprinkleroom to the railway station, as good as new, so their menfolk completed the appointed term of labour service and ventured forth to claim them, on the ramp, a trifle dishevelled to be sure, but strong and sleek from their regime of hard work and strict diet. As matchmakers, we didn't know the meaning of the word *failure*; on the ramp, stunning successes were as cheap as spit. When the families coalesced, how their hands and eyes would plead for one another, under our indulgent gaze. We toasted them far into the night. One guard, his knees bent and swaying, played an accordion. Actually we all drank like fiends. The stag party on the ramp, and the *kapos*, like the groom's best friends shoving the man into the waiting cart—freshly sprayed with trash and shit—for the journey home.

The Auschwitz universe, it has to be allowed, was fiercely copracentric. It was *made* of shit. In the early months I still had my natural aversion to overcome, before I understood the fundamental strangeness of the process of fruition. Enlightenment was urged on me the day I saw the old Jew float to the surface of the deep latrine, how he splashed and struggled into life, and was hoisted out by the jubilant guards, his clothes cleansed by the mire. Then they put his beard back on. I also found it salutary to watch the *Scheissekommando* about its work. This team had the job of replenishing the ditches from the soil wagon, not with buckets or anything like that but with flat wooden spades. In fact a great many of the camp's labour programmes were quite clearly unproductive. They weren't destructive either. Fill that hole. Dig it up again. Shift that. Then shift it back. Therapy was the order of the day . . . The *Scheissekommando* was made up of our most cultured patients: academics, rabbis, writers, philosophers. As they worked, they sang arias, and whistled scraps of symphonies, and recited poetry, and talked about Heine, and Schiller, and Goethe . . . In the officers' club, when we are drinking (which we nearly always are), and where shit is constantly mentioned and invoked, we sometimes refer to Auschwitz as Anus Mundi. And I can think of no finer tribute than that.

I have started corresponding with my wife, whose name is Herta. Herta's letters come, not from the fire (*das Feuer*), but from the trash (*der Plunder*). And they are in German. My letters to Herta are brought to me by the valet. I laboriously erase them, here, at night, in the silent room. I am left with nice sheets of white paper. But what for? My letters are in German too, though they contain gobbets of English which are playfully pedagogic in tone. I think it makes sense that Herta and I should get to know each other in this way. We're pen pals.

It seems that my wife has already conceived her doubts about the work we are doing here.

'Uncle Pepi' was everywhere. This being the thing that was most often said about him. For instance, 'It's as if he's everywhere,' or 'The man seems to be everywhere,' or, more simply, '"Uncle Pepi" is everywhere.' Omnipresence was only one of several attributes that tipped him over into the realm of the superhuman: he was also fantastically clean, for Auschwitz; when he was present, and he was present everywhere, I could sense the various cuts and nicks on my queasy jawline, my short but disobedient hair, the unhappy hang of my uniform, my lustreless black boots. His face was feline in shape, wide at the temples, and his blink was as slow as any cat's. On the ramp he cut a frankly glamorous figure, where he moved like a series of elegant decisions. You felt that he was only playing the part of a human being. Self-isolated as he was, 'Uncle Pepi' none the less displayed the best kind of condescension, and was in fact unusually collegial—not so much with youngsters like myself, of course, but with more senior medical figures, like Thilo and Wirths. I was moreover privileged—and on something like a regular basis—to assist 'Uncle Pepi' in Room 1 on Block 20, and later in Block 10 itself.

I recognized Room 1 from my dreams. The pink rubber apron on its hook, the instrument bowls and thermoses, the bloody cotton, the half-pint hypodermic with its foot-long needle. This is the room, I had thought, where something mortal would be miserably decided. But dreams are playful, and love to tease and poke fun at the truth . . . Already showing signs of life, patients were brought in one by one from the pile next door and wedged on to the chair in Room 1, which looked like what it was, a laboratory in the Hygienic Institute, a world of bubbles and bottles. With the syringe there were two ways to go, intravenous and cardiac, 'Uncle Pepi' tending to champion the latter as more efficient and humane. We did both. Cardiac: the patient blindfolded with a towel, his right hand placed in the mouth to stifle his own whimpers, the needle eased in to the dramatic trough of the fifth rib space. Intravenous: the patient with his forearm on the support table, the rubber tourniquet, the visible vein, the needle, the judicious dab of alcohol. 'Uncle Pepi' was then sometimes obliged to bring them to their senses with a few slaps about the face. The corpses were pink and blue-bruised. Death was pink but yellowish, and contained in a glass cylinder labelled PHENOL. A day of that and you stroll out in your white coat and black boots, with the familiar headache and the plangent perfecto and the breakfast tannic gathering in your throat, and the eastward sky looked like phenol.

He led. We followed. Phenol work became absolutely routine. All of us did it the whole time. It wasn't until later that I saw what 'Uncle Pepi' was capable of, in Block 10.

My wife Maria paid her first visit to Auschwitz in the spring of 1944, which was perhaps unfortunate: we were then doing the Hungarian Jews, and at an incredible rate, something like 10,000 a day. Unfortunate, because I was on ramp duty practically every night, finding the work somewhat impersonal too, the *selections* now being made by loudspeaker (such was the weight of the traffic), and having little to do but stand there drinking and shouting with my colleagues—thus denying Maria the kind of undivided attention that every young wife craves . . . Wait. Let me go at this another way.

Everything was ready for her. With typical sensitivity, Dr Wirths had made available the annex of his own living quarters—a delightful apartment (with its own kitchen and bathroom) beyond whose patterned lace curtains stood a high white fence. Beyond that, unseen, the benign cacophony of the Lager. I had been sitting on the sofa, quietly weeping; but I stood to attention when I heard the staff car approach, and walked out briskly to the little front garden. What did I expect? The usual awkwardness, I suppose. Reproaches, accusations, sadness—perhaps obscenities, even feeble blows from feeble fists. All to be at least partly resolved, that same night, in the act of love. That's how these things *usually* begin. What I didn't expect was the truth. The truth was the last thing I was ready for. I should have known. The world, after all, here in Auschwitz, has a new habit of making sense.

The driver looked on solemnly as she alighted from the staff car and started down the path. Then she turned to confront me. She looked nothing like her photograph. There was no vigour or certainty in her face.

'I don't know you,' she said. *Kennen*: know, be acquainted with.

'Please,' I said.

'You are a stranger to me.' *Fremder*: stranger.

'Please,' I said. 'My darling.' *Bitte. Liebling.*

Maria kept her head dipped as I helped her off with her coat. And something enveloped me, something that was all ready for my measurements, like a suit or a uniform, over and above what I wore, and lined with grief. I felt it tighten around me.

With the war going so well now, and with the slight decline in the workload after the feats of '44, and with the general burgeoning of confidence and wellbeing, why, the camp doctor is agreeably surprised to find the time and leisure to pursue his hobbies. The Soviet trogs have been driven back into their frozen potholes: the camp doctor steadies his monocle and reaches for his mustiest textbook. Or his binoculars and shooting-stick. Whatever. Depending on natural bent. Winter was cold but autumn is come—the stubble fields, and so on. The simpering Vistula. In one of her baffling letters Maria goes so far as to question the *legality* of the work we are doing here! Well. Let me see . . . I suppose you *could* say that there are one or two 'gray areas'. Block 11, the Black Wall, the measures of the Political Unit: these excite some controversy. And, should a patient take matters into his own hands, with the electric fence for example, there's certainly no end of a palaver. We all *hate* that . . . I am famed for my quiet dedication. The other doctors disappear for weeks at a stretch; but in the summer air of the Kat-Zet I have no need of *Sommerfrische*. I do love the feel of the sun on my face, it's true. 'Uncle Pepi' has really surpassed himself with his new laboratory: the marble table, the nickel taps, the porcelain sinks. Provincial: that's the word for Maria. You know, of course, that she doesn't even shave her legs? The armpit question will remain eternally arguable, but the legs, surely, the legs . . . In this new lab of his he can knock together a human being out of the unlikeliest odds and ends. On his desk he had a box full of eyes. It was not uncommon to see him slipping out of his darkroom carrying a head partly wrapped in an old newspaper. Extra bones and brains were sent to him from Berlin, where Maria lives. The next thing you knew, there'd be, oh, I don't know, a fifteen-year-old Pole sliding off the table and sauntering back to work, accompanied by an orderly and his easy-going smile. It would be criminal—it would be criminal to neglect the opportunity which Auschwitz affords for the furtherance . . . I see him at the wheel of his Mercedes-Benz, on the day that the gypsy camp was established, personally ferrying the children from the central hospital. The gypsy camp, its rosy pinks, its dirty prettiness. '"Uncle Pepi"! "Uncle Pepi"!' the children cried. When was that? When did we do the gypsy camp? Before the Czech family camp? Yes. Oh, long ago. Maria came again. Her second visit could not be accounted a success, though we were much more intimate than before, and wept a lot together about the baby. As to the so-called 'experimental' operations of 'Uncle Pepi': *he* had a success rate that approached—and quite possibly attained—100 per cent. A shockingly inflamed eyeball at once rectified by a single injection. Innumerable ovaries and testes seamlessly grafted into place. We can make another baby, Maria and I. If I wept copiously both before and after, she let me do it, or try it, but I am impotent and don't even go to the whore any more. I have no power. I have no power. 'Uncle Pepi' never left any scars. You know, it isn't all sweetness and light here, not by any manner of means. *Some of the patients were doctors*, and it wasn't long before they were up to their old tricks. I am prominent in the campaign against this scum. The baby will be here soon and I feel very concerned. 'Uncle Pepi' is right: I do need a holiday. But my visit to Berlin for the funeral is mercifully brief: the drizzling parquetry of the streets, the shoplights like the valves of an old radio, the drenched churchyard, the skin and weight problems of the young cleric, Maria's parents, Maria's hideous face. There is a war on, I keep telling everyone. We are in the front line. What are we fighting? Phenol? On my return from Berlin to the light and space of Auschwitz what should await me but a telegram. The baby is very weak, and I should come at once, and the doctors have done all they can. The casket was about 15" by 20". But I am fighting the phenol war, and thanklessly. No one shows me any gratitude. I seem to have developed a respiratory difficulty—stress asthma, perhaps—particularly when I am shouting. In the Sprinkleroom, when the guards touch the girls, and I repeatedly register my objections, the men mime the playing of violins. They think, because I am a husband and father, that I have become sentimental. I long to see my little Eva, of course, but the present situation is counterindicative. I have stopped going to the bordello but at least I now know why I went there: for the gratitude. Those patient-doctors are getting quite out of hand. They make me choke with rage. For some reason they show a special zeal in interfering with the children; how wanton and gratuitous this interference feels, when you consider that the children, after all, won't be around for very long. I am not in it for the gratitude. I am in it—if you want a *why*—because I love the human body and all living things. It isn't just phenol, not any more. In that sense the war front has widened. It is a war on death that comes in many forms. As well as phenol we now extract prussic acid and sodium evipan. You sense a rushing eagerness when completion is near and there are souls still stacked like desperate aeroplanes circling above an airport. Some exceptions should be duly noted: an old man hugging and kissing my black boots; a child clinging to me as I held her down for 'Uncle Pepi'. But not once did I receive what might be described as sober and reasoned thanks. I am not complaining. But it would have been nice. As well as prussic acid and sodium evipan we now extract benzene, gasoline, kerosene and air. Yes, air! Human beings want to be alive. They are dying to be alive. Twenty cc's of air—of nothing—is all you need to make the difference. So nobody thanks me as, with a hypodermic almost the size of a trombone and my right foot firmly stamped on the patient's chest, I continue to prosecute the war against air.

GRANTA

T. CORAGHESSAN BOYLE
SITTING ON TOP OF THE WORLD

People would ask her what it was like. She'd watch them from her tower as they weaved along the trail in their baseball caps and day packs, their shorts, hiking boots and sneakers. The brave ones would mount the 150 wooden steps hammered into the face of the mountain to stand at the highflown railing of the little glass-walled shack she called home for seven months a year. Sweating, sucking at canteens and bota bags, heaving for breath in the undernourished air, they would ask her what it was like. 'Beautiful,' she would say. 'Peaceful.'

But that didn't begin to express it. It was like floating untethered, drifting with the clouds, like being cupped in the hands of God. Nine thousand feet up, she could see the distant hazy rim of the world, she could see Mt Whitney rising up above the crenellations of the Sierra, she could see stars that haven't been discovered yet. In the morning, she was the first to watch the sun emerge from the hills to the east, and in the evening, when it was dark beneath her, the valleys and ridges gripped by the insinuating fingers of the night, she was the last to see it set. There was the wind in the trees, the murmur of the infinite needles soughing in the uncountable branches of the pines, sequoias and cedars that stretched out below her like a carpet. There was daybreak. There was the stillness of three a.m. She couldn't explain it. She was sitting on top of the world.

Don't you get lonely up here? they'd ask. Don't you get a little stir-crazy?

And how to explain that? Yes, she did, of course she did, but it didn't matter. Todd was up here with her in the summer, one week on, one week off, and then the question was meaningless. But in September he went back to the valley, to his father, to school, and the world began to drag round its tired old axis. The hikers stopped coming then too. In the height of summer, on a weekend, she'd see as many as thirty or forty in the course of a day, but now, with the fall coming on, they left her to herself—sometimes she'd go for days without seeing a soul.

But that was the point, wasn't it?

She was making breakfast—a real breakfast for a change, ham and eggs from the propane refrigerator, fresh-dripped coffee and toast—when she spotted him working his way along one of the switchbacks below. She was immediately annoyed. It wasn't even seven yet and the sign at the trailhead quite plainly stated that visitors were welcome at the lookout between the hours of ten and five *only*. What was wrong with this guy—did he think he was exempt or something? She calmed herself: maybe he was only crossing the trail. Deer season had opened—she'd been hearing the distant muted pop of gunfire all week—and maybe he was only a hunter tracking a deer.

No such luck. When she glanced down again, flipping her eggs, peering across the face of the granite peak and the steep snaking trail that clung to it, she saw that he was coming up to the tower. Damn, she thought, and then the kettle began to hoot and her stomach clenched. Breakfast was ruined. Now there'd be some stranger gawking over her shoulder and making the usual banal comments as she ate. To them it might have been like Disneyland or something up here, but this was her home, she lived here. How would they like it if she showed up on their doorstep at seven o'clock in the morning?

She was eating, her back to the glass door, hoping he'd go away, slip over the lip of the precipice and disappear, vanish in a puff of smoke, when she felt his footfall on the trembling catwalk that ran round the outside of the tower. Still, she didn't turn or look up. She was reading—she went through a truckload of books in the course of a season—and she never lifted her eyes from the page. He could gawk round the catwalk, peer through the telescope and hustle himself back on down the steps for all she cared. She wasn't a tour guide. Her job was to watch for smoke, twenty-four hours a day, and to be cordial—if she was in the mood and had the time—to the hikers who made the sweaty panting trek in from the trailhead to join her for a brief moment atop the world. There was no law that said she had to let them in the shack or show them the radio and her plotting equipment and deliver the standard lecture on how it all worked. Especially at seven in the morning. To hell with him, she thought, and she forked up egg and tried to concentrate on her book.

The problem was, she'd trained herself to look up from what she was doing and scan the horizon every thirty seconds or so, day or night, except when she was asleep, and it had become a reflex. She glanced up, and there he was. It gave her a shock. He'd gone round the catwalk to the far side and he was standing right in front of her, grinning and holding something up to the window. Flowers, wildflowers, she registered that, but then his face came into focus and she felt something go slack in her: she knew him. He'd been here before.

'Lainie,' he said, tapping the glass and brandishing the flowers, 'I brought you something.'

Her name. He knew her name.

She tried a smile and her face froze around it. The book on the table before her upset the salt shaker and flipped itself shut with a tiny expiring hiss. Should she thank him? Should she get up and latch the door? Should she put out an emergency call on the radio and snatch up the kitchen knife?

'Sorry to disturb you over breakfast—I didn't know the time,' he said, and something happened to his grin, though his eyes—a hard metallic blue—held on to hers like pincers. He raised his voice to penetrate the glass: 'I've been camping down on Long Meadow Creek and when I crossed the trail this morning I just thought you might be lonely and I'd surprise you'—he hesitated—'I mean, with some flowers.'

Her whole body was frozen now. She'd had crazies up here before—it was an occupational hazard—but there was something unnerving about this one, this one she remembered. 'It's too early,' she said finally, miming it with her hands, as if the glass were impervious to sound, and then she got up from her untouched ham and half-eaten eggs and deliberately went to the radio. The radio was just under the window where he was standing and when she picked up the mike and depressed the talk button she was two feet from him, the thin wall of glass all that separated them.

'Needles Lookout,' she said, 'this is Elaine. Zack, you there? Over.'

Zack's voice came right back at her. He was a college student working on a degree in forestry, and he was her relief two days a week when she hiked out and went down the mountain to spend a day with her son, do her shopping and maybe hit a bar or movie with her best friend and soulmate, Cynthia Furman. 'Elaine,' he said, above the crackle of static, 'what's up? See anything funny out there? Over.'

She forced herself to look up then and locate the stranger's eyes—he was still grinning, but the grin was slack and unsteady and there was no joy in the deeps of those hard blue eyes—and she held the black plastic mike to her lips a moment longer than she had to before answering. 'Nothing, Zack,' she said, 'just checking in.'

His voice was tinny. 'OK,' he said. 'Talk to you. Over and out.'

'Over and out,' she said.

And now what? The guy wore a hunting knife strapped to his thigh. His cheeks were caved in as if he were sucking candy and an old-fashioned moustache, thick and reddish, hid his upper lip. Instead of a baseball cap he wore a wide-brimmed felt hat. Wyatt Earp, she thought, and she was about to turn away from the window, prepared to ignore him till he took the hint, till he counted off the 150 wooden steps and vanished down the path and out of her life, when he rapped again on the glass and said, 'You got something to put these in—the flowers, I mean?'

She didn't want his flowers. She didn't want him on her platform. She didn't want him in her 13' by 13' sanctuary, touching her things, poking around, asking stupid questions, making small talk. 'Look,' she said finally, talking to the glass but looking through him, beyond him, scanning the infinite as she'd trained herself to do, no matter what the problem, 'I've got a job to do up here and the fact is no one's allowed on the platform between the hours of five in the afternoon and ten in the morning'—now she came back to him and saw that his smile had collapsed—'you ought to know that. It says so in plain English right down there at the trailhead.' She looked away, it was over, she was done with him.

She went back to her breakfast, forcing herself to stare at the page before her, though her heart was going and the words meant nothing. Todd had been with her the first time the man had come. Todd was fourteen, tall like his father, blond-headed and rangy. He was a good kid, her last and final hope, and he seemed to relish the time he spent with her up here. It was a Saturday, the middle of the afternoon, and they'd had a steady stream of visitors since the morning. Todd was in the storage room below, reading comics (in its wisdom, the Forestry Service had provided this second room, twenty-five steps down, not simply for storage but for respite too—it was a box, a womb, with only a single dull high-placed window to light it, antithesis and antidote to the naked glass box above). Elaine was at her post, chopping vegetables for soup and scanning the horizon.

She hadn't noticed him coming—there'd been so many visitors she wasn't attuned to them in the way she was in the quiet times. She was feeling hospitable, light-hearted, the hostess of an on-going party. There'd been a professor up earlier, an ornithologist, and they'd had a long talk about the golden eagle and the red-tailed hawk. And then there was the young girl from Merced—she couldn't have been more than seventeen—with her baby strapped to her back, and two heavy-set women in their sixties who'd proudly made the two and a half mile trek in from the trailhead and were giddy with the thin air and the thrill of their own accomplishment. Elaine had offered them each a cup of tea, not wanting to spoil their fun and point out that it was still two and a half miles back out.

She'd felt his weight on the platform and turned to give him a smile. He was tall and powerful across the chest and shoulders and he'd tipped his hat to her and poked his head in the open door. 'Enjoying the view?' he said.

There was something in his eyes that should have warned her off, but she was feeling sociable and buoyant and she saw the generosity in his shoulders and hands. 'It's nothing compared to the Ventura Freeway,' she deadpanned.

He laughed out loud at that, and he was leaning in the door now, both hands on the frame. 'I see the monastic life hasn't hurt your sense of humour any—' and then he paused, as if he'd gone too far. 'Or that's not the word I want, "monastic"—is there a feminine version of that?'

Pretty presumptuous. Flirtatious too. But she was in the

mood, she didn't know what it was—maybe having Todd with her, maybe just the sheer bubbling joy of living on the crest of the sky—and at least he wasn't dragging her through the same old tired conversation about loneliness and beauty and smoke on the horizon she had to endure about a hundred times a week. 'Come in,' she said. 'Take a load off your feet.'

He sat on the edge of the bed and removed his hat. He wore his hair in a modified punk style—hard irregular spikes—and that surprised her: somehow it just didn't go with the cowboy hat. His jeans were stiff and new and his tooled boots looked as if they'd just been polished. He was studying her—she was wearing khaki shorts and a T-shirt, she'd washed her hair that morning in anticipation of the crowd, and her legs were good—she knew it—tanned and shaped by her treks up and down the trail. She felt something she hadn't felt in a long time, an ice age, and she knew her cheeks were flushed. 'You probably had a whole slew of visitors today, huh?' he said, and there was something incongruous in the enforced folksiness of the phrase, something that didn't go with his accent, just as the haircut didn't go with the hat.

'I've counted twenty-six since this morning.' She diced a carrot, tossed it into the pan to simmer with the onions and zucchini she'd chopped a moment earlier.

He was gazing out the window, working his hands on the brim of his hat. 'Hope you don't mind my saying this, but you're the best thing about this view as far as I can see. You're pretty. Really pretty.'

This one she'd heard before. About a thousand times. Probably seventy per cent of the day-trippers who made the hike out to the lookout were male, and, if they were alone or with other males, about ninety per cent of those tried to hit on her in some way. She resented it, but she couldn't blame them really. There was probably something irresistible in the formula: young woman with blonde hair and good legs in a glass tower in the middle of nowhere—and all alone. Rapunzel, let down your hair. Usually she deflected the compliment—or the moves—by turning officious, standing on her authority as Forestry Service employee, government servant and the chief, queen and despot of the

Needles Lookout. This time she said nothing. Just lifted her head for a quick scan of the horizon and then looked back down at the knife and the cutting board and began chopping green onion and cilantro.

He was still watching her. The bed was big, a double, one of the few creature comforts the Forestry Service provided up here. There was no headboard, of course—just a big flat hard slab of mattress attached to the wall at window level, so you could be lying in bed and still do your job. Presumably, it was designed for couples. When he spoke again, she knew what he was going to say before the words were out of his mouth. 'Nice bed,' he said.

What did she expect? He was no different from the rest—why would he be? All of a sudden he'd begun to get on her nerves, and when she turned her face to him her voice was cold. 'Have you seen the telescope?' she said, indicating the Bushnell Televar mounted on the rail of the catwalk—beyond the window and out the door.

He ignored her. He rose to his feet. Thirteen by thirteen: two's a crowd. 'You must get awfully lonely up here,' he said, and his voice was different now too, no attempt at folksiness or jocularity, 'a pretty woman like you. A beautiful woman. You've got sexy legs, you know that?'

She flushed—he could see that, she was sure of it—and the flush made her angry. She was about to tell him off, to tell him to get the hell out of her house and stay out, when Todd came rumbling up the steps, wild-eyed and excited. 'Mom!' he shouted, and he was out of breath, his voice high-pitched and hoarse, 'there's water leaking all over the place out there!'

Water. It took a moment to register. The water was precious up here, irreplaceable. Once a month two bearded men with Forestry Service patches on their sleeves brought her six twenty-gallon containers of it—in the old way, on the backs of mules. She husbanded that water as if she were in the middle of the Negev, every drop of it, rarely allowing herself the luxury of a quick shampoo and rinse, as she had that morning. In the next instant she was out the door and jolting down the steps behind her son. Down below, outside the storage room where the cartons were lined up in a straight standing row, she saw that the rock face was slick with a finely spread sheen of water. She bent to the near carton. It was leaking from a thin milky stress fracture in the plastic, an inch from the bottom. 'Take hold of it, Todd,' she said, 'we've got to turn it over so the leak's on top.'

Full, the carton weighed better than 160 pounds, and this one was nearly full. She put her weight behind it, the power of her honed and muscular legs, but the best she could do, even with Todd's help, was to push the thing over on its side. She was breathing hard, sweating, she'd scraped her knee and there was a stipple of blood on the skin over the kneecap. It was then that she became aware of the stranger standing there behind her. She looked up at him framed against the vastness of the sky, the sun in his face, his big hands on his hips. 'Need a hand there?' he asked.

Looking back on it, she didn't know why she'd refused—maybe it was the way Todd gaped at him in awe, maybe it was the old pretty woman/lonely up here routine or the helpless female syndrome—but before she could think she was saying 'I don't need your help: I can do it myself.'

And then his hands fell from his hips and he backed away a step, and suddenly he was apologetic, he was smooth and funny and winning and he was sorry for bothering her and he just wanted to help and he knew she was capable, he wasn't implying anything—and just as suddenly he caught himself, dropped his shoulders and slunk off down the steps without another word.

For a long moment she watched him receding down the trail, and then she turned back to the water container. By the time she and Todd got it upended it was half empty.

Yes. And now he was here when he had no right to be, now he was intruding and he knew it, now he was a crazy defining new levels of the affliction. She'd call in an emergency in a second—she wouldn't hesitate—and they'd have a helicopter here in less than five minutes, that's how quick these firefighters were, she'd seen them in action. Five minutes. She wouldn't hesitate. She kept her head down. She cut and chewed each piece of meat with slow deliberation and she read and re-read the same paragraph until it lost all sense. When she looked up, he was gone.

After that, the day dragged on as if it would never end. He couldn't have been there more than ten minutes, slouching around with his mercenary grin and his pathetic flowers, but he'd managed to ruin her day. He'd upset her equilibrium and she found that she couldn't read, couldn't sketch or work on the sweater she was knitting for Todd. She caught herself staring at a fixed point on the horizon, drifting, her mind a blank. She ate too much. Lunch was a ceremony, dinner a ritual. There were no visitors, though for once she longed for them. Dusk lingered in the western sky and when night fell she didn't bother with her propane lantern but merely sat there on the corner of the bed, caught up in the wheeling immensity of the constellations and the dream of the Milky Way.

And then she couldn't sleep. She kept thinking of him, the stranger with the big hands and secretive eyes, kept scanning the catwalk for the sudden black shadow of him. If he came at seven in the morning, why not at three? What was to prevent him? There was no sound, nothing—the wind had died down and the night was clear and moonless. For the first time since she'd been here, for the first time in three long seasons, she felt naked and vulnerable, exposed in her glass house like a fish in a tank. The night was everything and it held her in its grip.

She thought about Mike then, about the house they'd had when Mike had finished his degree and started as an assistant professor at a little state school out in the lost lush hills of Oregon. The house was an A-frame, a cabin with a loft, set down amidst the trees like a cottage in a fairy tale. It was all windows and everywhere you looked the trees bowed down and stepped into the house. The previous owner, an old widower with watery eyes and yellow hair climbing out of his ears, hadn't bothered with blinds or curtains, and Mike didn't like that—he was always after her to measure the windows and order blinds or buy the material for drapes. She'd balked. The openness, the light, the sense of connection and belonging: these were the things that had attracted her in the first place. They made love in the dark—Mike insisted on it—as if it were something to be ashamed of. After a while, it was.

Then she was thinking of a time before that, a time before

Todd and graduate school, when Mike sat with her in the dormitory lounge, books spread out on the coffee-table before them, the heat and murmur of a dozen other couples locking their mouths and bodies together. A study date. For hours she clung to him, the sofa like a boat pitching in a heavy sea, the tease of it, the fumbling innocence, the interminable foreplay that left her wet and itching while the wind screamed beyond the iced-over windows. That was something. The R.A. would flash the lights and it was quarter of two and they would fling themselves at each other, each step to the door drenched in hormones, sticky with them, desperate, until finally he was gone and she felt the loss like a war bride. Until the next night.

Finally, and it must have been two, three in the morning, the Big Dipper tugged down below the horizon, Orion looming overhead, she thought of the stranger who'd spoiled her breakfast. He'd sat there on the corner of the bed, he'd stood beyond the window with his sad bundle of flowers, devouring the sky. As she thought of him, in that very moment, there was a dull light thump on the steps, a faint rustle, movement, and she couldn't breathe, couldn't move. The seconds pounded in her head and the rustling—it was like the sweep of a broom—was gone, something in the night, a pack rat, the fleeting touch of an owl's wing. She thought of those hands, the eyes, the square of those shoulders, and she felt herself being drawn down into the night in relief, and finally, in gratitude.

She woke late, the sun slanting across the floor to touch her lips and mask her eyes. Zachary was on the radio with the news that Oakland had clinched the pennant and a hurricane was tearing up the East Coast. 'You sound awful,' he said. 'I didn't wake you, did I?'

'I couldn't sleep.'

'Star-gazing again, huh?'

She tried out a laugh for him. 'I guess,' she said. There was a silence. 'Jesus, you just relieved me. I've got four more days to put in before I come back down to the ground.'

'Just don't get mystical on me. And leave me some granola this time, will you? And if you run out, call me. That's my breakfast we're talking about. And lunch. And sometimes, if I don't feel like cooking—'

She cut him off: 'Dinner. I know. I will.' She yawned. 'Talk to you.'

'Yeah. Over and out.'

'Over and out.'

When she set the kettle on the grill there was gas, but when she turned her back to dig the butter out of the refrigerator, the flame was gone. She tried another match, but there was nothing. That meant she had to switch propane tanks, a minor nuisance. The tanks, which were flown in once a year by helicopter, were located at the base of the stairway, 150 steps down. There was a flat spot there, a gap cut into the teeth of the outcrop and overhung on one side by a sloping twenty-foot high wall of rock. On the other side, the first step was a thousand feet down.

She shrugged into her shorts, and because it was cold despite the sun—she'd seen snow as early as the fifth of September and the month was almost gone now—she pulled on an oversized sweater that had once belonged to Mike. After she moved out she found it in a pillowcase she'd stuffed full of clothes. He hadn't wanted it back. It was windy and a blast knifed into her when she threw open the door and started down the steps. Big pristine tufts of cumulus hurried across the sky, swelling and attenuating and changing shape, but she didn't see anything dark enough—or big enough—to portend a storm. Still, you could never tell. The breeze was from the north and the radio had reported a storm front moving in off the Pacific—it really wouldn't surprise her to see snow on the ground by this time tomorrow. A good snowfall and the fire season would be over and she could go home. Early.

She thought about that, about the four walls of the little efficiency she rented on a dead street in a dead town to be near Todd during the winter, and hoped it wouldn't snow. Not now. Not yet. In a dry year—and this had been the third dry year in a row—she could stay through mid-November. She reached the bottom of the steps and crouched over the propane tanks, two 300 gallon jobs painted Forestry Service green, feeling depressed over the thought of those four dull walls and the cold in the air and the storm that might or might not develop. There was gooseflesh on her legs and her breath crowded the air round her. She watched a ground squirrel, its shoulders bulky with patches of bright grey fur, dart up over the face of the overhang, and then she unfastened the coupling on the empty tank and switched the hose to the full one.

'Gas problems?'

The voice came from above and behind her and she jumped as if she'd been stung. Even before she whirled round she knew whose voice it was.

'Hey, hey: didn't meant to startle you. Whoa. Sorry.' There he was, the happy camper, knife lashed to his thigh, standing right behind her, two steps up. This time his eyes were hidden behind a pair of reflecting sunglasses. The brim of the Stetson was pulled down low and he wore a sheepskin coat, the fleecy collar turned up in back.

She couldn't answer. Couldn't smile. Couldn't humour him. He'd caught her out of her sanctuary, caught her out in the open, 150 steep and unforgiving steps from the radio, the kitchen knife, the hard flat soaring bed. She was crouching. He towered above her, his shoulders cut out of the sky. Todd was in school. Mike—she didn't want to think about Mike. She was all alone.

He stood there, the moustache the only thing alive in his face. It lifted from his teeth in a grin. 'Those things can be a pain,' he said, the folksy tone creeping into his voice, 'those tanks, I mean. Dangerous. I use electricity myself.'

She lifted herself cautiously from her crouch, the hard muscles swelling in her legs. She would have risked a dash up the stairs, all 150 of them, would have put her confidence in her legs, but he was blocking the stairway—almost as if he'd anticipated her. She hadn't said a word yet. She looked scared, she knew it. 'Still camping?' she said, fighting to open up her face and give him his smile back, insisting on banality, normalcy, the meaningless drift of meaningless conversation.

He looked away from her, light flashing from the slick convexity of the sunglasses, and kicked at the edge of the step with the silver-tipped toe of his boot. After a moment he turned back to her and removed the sunglasses. 'Yeah,' he said, shrugging. 'I guess.'

It wasn't an answer she expected. He guessed? What was that supposed to mean? He hadn't moved a muscle and he was watching her with that look in his eyes—she knew that look, knew that stance, that moustache and hat, but she didn't know his name. He knew hers but she didn't know his, not even his first name. 'I'm sorry,' she said, and when she put a hand up to her eyes to shade them from the sun, it was trembling, 'but what was your name again? I mean, I remember you, of course, not just from yesterday but from that time a month or so ago, but . . .' she trailed off.

He didn't seem to have heard her. The wind sang in the trees. She just stood there, squinting into the sun—there was nothing else she could do. 'I wasn't camping, not really,' he said. 'Not that I don't love the wilderness—and I do camp, backpack and all that—but I just—I thought that's what you'd want to hear.'

What she'd want to hear? What was he talking about? She stole a glance at the tower, sun flashing the windows, clouds pricked on the peak of the roof, and it seemed as distant as the stars at night. If she were only up there she'd put out an emergency, she would, she'd have them here in five minutes . . .

'Actually,' and he looked away now, his shoulders slumping in that same hangdog way they had when she'd refused his help with the water carton, 'actually I've got a cabin up on Cedar Slope. I just, I just thought you'd want to hear I was camping.' He'd been staring down at the toe of his boots, but suddenly he looked up at her and grinned till his back fillings glinted in the light. 'I think Elaine's a pretty name, did I tell you that?'

'Thank you,' she said, almost against her will, and softly, so softly she could barely hear it herself. He could rape her here, he could kill her, anything. Was that what he wanted? Was that it? 'Listen,' she said, pushing it, she couldn't help herself, 'listen, I've got to get back to work—'

'I know, I know,' he said, holding up the big slab of his hand, 'back to the nest, huh? I know I must be a pain in the—in the butt for you, and I'll bet I'm not the first one to say it, but you're just too good-looking a woman to be wasted out here on the squirrels and coyotes.' He stepped down, stepped towards her, and she thought in that instant of trying to dart past him, a wild thought, instinctual and desperate, a thought that clawed its way into her brain and froze there before she could move. 'Jesus,' he said, and his voice was harsh with conviction, 'don't you get lonely?'

And then she saw it, below and to the right, movement, two bobbing pink hunter's caps, coming up the trail. It was over. Just like that. She could walk away from him, mount the stairs, lock herself in the tower. But why was her heart still going, why did she feel as if it hadn't even begun? 'Damn,' she said, directing her gaze, 'more visitors. Now I really have to get back.'

He followed her eyes and looked down to where the hunters sank out of view and then bobbed back up again, working their way up the path. She could see their faces now—two men, middle-aged, wispy hair sticking out from beneath the fluorescent caps. No guns. Cameras. He studied them a moment and then looked into her eyes, looked deep, as if he'd lost something. Then he shrugged, turned his back and started down the path toward them.

She was in good shape, the best shape of her life. She'd been up the steps a thousand times, two thousand, but she'd never climbed them quicker than she did now. She flew up the stairs like something blown by the wind and she felt a kind of panic beating against her ribs and she smelled the storm coming and felt the cold to the marrow of her bones. And then she reached the door and slammed it shut behind her, fumbling for the latch. It was then, only then, that she noticed the flowers. They were in the centre of the table, in a cut-glass vase, lupin, groundsel, forget-me-not.

It snowed in the night, monstrous swirling oversized flakes that clawed at the windows and filled her with despair. The lights would only have made her feel vulnerable and exposed and for the second night running she did without them, sitting there in the dark, cradling the kitchen knife and listening for his footfall on the steps while the sky fell to pieces around her. But he wouldn't come, not in this weather, not at night—she was being foolish, childish, there was nothing to worry about. Except the snow. It meant that her season was over. And if her season was over, she had to go back down the mountain and into the real world, real time, into the smog and roar and clutter.

She thought of the four walls that awaited her, the hopeless job—waitressing or fast food or some such slow crucifixion of the spirit—and she thought of Mike before she left him, saw him there in the black glass of the window, sexless, pale, the little butterfly-wing bifocals perched on the tip of his nose, pecking at the typewriter, pecking, pecking, in love with Dryden, Swift, Pope, in love with dead poets, in love with death itself. She'd met a man at a party a month after she'd left him and he was just like Mike, only he was in love with arthropods. Arthropods. And then she came up to the tower.

She woke late again and the first thing she felt was relief. The sun was out and the snow—it was only a dusting, nothing really—had already begun to recede from the naked high crown of the rock. She put on the kettle and went to the radio. 'Zack,' she called, 'Needle Rock. Do you copy?'

He was there, right at her fingertips. 'Copy. Over.'

'We had some snow up here—nothing much, just a dusting really. It's clear now.'

'You're a little late—Lewis already checked in from Mule Peak with that information. Oversleep again?'

'Yeah, I guess so.' She was watching the distant treetops shake off the patina of snow. A hawk sailed across the window. She held the microphone so close to her lips it could have been a part of her. 'Zack—' she wanted to tell him about the crazy, about the man in the Stetson, about his hands, wanted to alert him just in case, but she hesitated. Her voice was tiny, detached, lost in the electronic crackle of time and space.

'Lainie?'

'Yes. Yes, I'm here.'

'There's a cold front coming through, another storm behind it. They're saying it could drop some snow. The season's still on—Reichert says it will be until we get appreciable precipitation—but this one could be it. It's up to you. You want to come out or wait and see?'

Reichert was the boss, fifty, bald, soft as a clam. The

mountains were parched—six inches of powdery duff covered the forest floor and half the creeks had run dry. The season could last till November. 'Wait and see,' she said.

'OK, it's your choice. Lewis is staying too, if it makes you feel better. I'll keep in touch if anything develops on this end.'

'Yeah. Thanks.'

'Over and out.'

'Over and out.'

It clouded over late in the afternoon and the sky closed in on her again. The temperature began to drop. It looked bad. It was early for snow yet, but they could get snow any time of the year at this altitude. The average was twenty-five feet annually, and she'd seen storms drop four and five feet at a time. She talked to Zack at four and he told her it looked pretty grim—they were calling for a seventy per cent chance of snow, with the snow level dropping to 3,000 feet. 'I'll take my chances,' she told him. There was a pair of snowshoes in the storage room if it came to that.

The snow started an hour later. She was cooking dinner—brown rice and vegetables—and she'd opened the bottle of wine she'd brought up to commemorate the last day of the season. The flakes were tiny, pellets that sifted down with a hiss, the sort of configuration that meant serious snow. The season was over. She could drink her wine and then think about packing up and cleaning the stove and refrigerator. She put another log on the woodstove and buttoned up her jacket.

The wine was half gone and she'd sat down to eat when she noticed the smoke. At first she thought it must be a trick of the wind, the smoke from her own stove twisting back on her. But no. Below her, no more than 500 feet, just about where the trail would be, she could see the flames. The wind blew a screen of snow across the window. There hadn't been any lightning—but there was a fire down there, she was sure of it. She got up from the table, snatched her binoculars from the hook by the door, and went out on the catwalk to investigate.

The wind took her breath away. All the universe had gone pale, white above and white beneath: she was perched on the clouds, living in them, diaphanous and ghostly. She could smell the smoke on the wind now. She lifted the binoculars to her eyes and the snow screened them; she tried again and her hair beat at the lenses. It took her a moment, but there, there it was: a fire leaping up out of the swirling grip of the snow. A campfire. But no, this was bigger, fallen trees stacked up in a pyramid—this was a bonfire, deliberate, this was a sign. The snow took it away from her. Her fingers were numb. When the fire came into focus again she saw movement there, a shadow leaping round the flames, feeding them, revelling in them, and she caught her breath. And then she saw the black jabbing peak of the Stetson and she understood.

He was camping.

Camping. He could die out there—he *was* crazy, he *was*—this thing could turn into a blizzard, it could snow for days. But he was camping. And then the thought came to her: he was camping for her.

Later, when the tower floated out over the storm and the coals glowed in the stove and the darkness settled in around her like a blanket, she disconnected the radio and put the knife away in the drawer where it belonged. Then she propped herself in the corner of the bed, way out over the edge of the abyss, and watched his fire raging in the cold heart of the night. He would be back, she knew that now, and she would be ready for him.

For most fringe venues, using the phrase "experimental theatre" on your publicity means the kiss of death at the box office. It joins "solo ventriloquist accompanied by performing dog" at the bottom of any list calculated to increase attendances beyond the local amateur stage correspondent.

Yet this is the theatre to which I'm passionately addicted. I'll travel miles for a ticket; freezing to death in an abandoned church to see IOU Theatre's glorious pageantry, tearful at Forced Entertainment's moving evocations of urban decay, outraged by the blatant confrontations of Dogs in Honey.

Of course not all of it works - it is experimental after all - but it's this risk-taking research and development wing of our theatre that, along with the contributions of other cultures, enriches and inspires the mainstream.

Try this experiment; take one friend - and go and see some!

Stella Hall
Chair of Arts Council Drama Projects

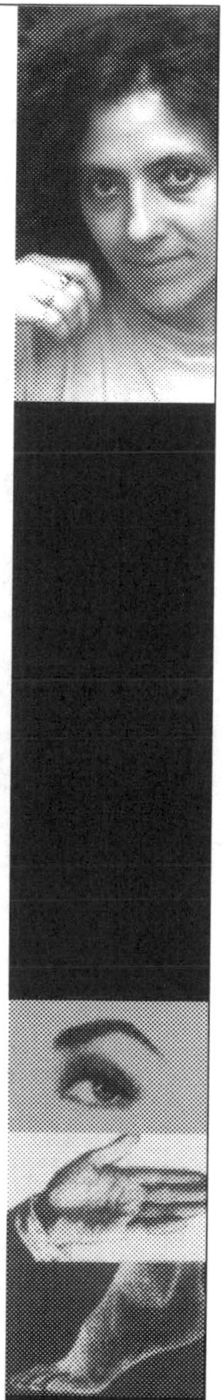

Barclays New Stages is a unique three-year sponsorship devised by Barclays Bank to encourage and promote fringe theatre. The scheme operates in two phases: the first offers sponsorship to original productions, the second supports a season at Britain;s leading venue for new writing - the Royal Court Theatre.

In its first year Barclays New Stages provided sponsorship to ten companies enabling them to create, perform and tour new works nationwide. Several of these companies, including Adventures in Motion Pictures, Dogs in Honey, Graeme Miller and Rose English, have been invited to perform at the first Barclays New Stages festival at the Royal Court Theatre which runs from 17 June to 13 July 1991.

Details of Barclays New Stages festival at the Royal Court Theatre, 071 730 1745

BARCLAYS
new stages

FOR INDEPENDENT THEATRE

GRANTA

Graham Swift

Plastic

FASHIONS
NYLONS

When I try to remember the glorious, the marvellous, the lost and luminous city of Paris, I find it hard to separate the city that exists in the mind, that existed even then, perhaps, mainly in my mind, from the actual city whose streets I once trod. We see what we choose to see, we see what we think we see. In Paris my mother first took me to the opera. A matinée of *La Bohème*—a Parisian tale. And there, in Act One, behind Rodolfo's garret window, and again, in Act Four, as poor Mimi lay melodiously dying, was a painted vista of Paris roof-tops just like any you could actually see, and perhaps still can, around Sacré Coeur or Montparnasse. It had never struck me before that Reality and Romance could so poignantly collude with each other; so that ever afterwards I saw Paris as a palpable network of 'scenes', down to the subtle lighting of a smoky-blue winter's morning or the blush of a spring evening; the incarnation of something already imagined. It scarcely occurred to me—my imagination did not go in this simpler direction—that this same Paris which we came to in November, 1945, had been occupied not so long ago by Hitler's soldiery and that our very apartment in the Rue de Bellechasse, in the heart of the ministerial quarter, had perhaps been the temporary home—as it was our temporary home—of some official of the Reich.

My mother (whom I would definitely not, in the final analysis, call Romantic) must have been moved by the same ambiguous, uncanny reality as me, because I can recall her, only days after our arrival, saying in a rapturous if half-startled voice, 'Look darling, this is Paris, darling,' (I knew it was Paris, we were in Paris, we were strolling down the Champs Elysées), 'isn't it divine?' And that word, through the refining filter of Paris, is all I need to conjure up my mother: as she flung the new Armstrong-Siddeley through the flashing, leafy lanes of Berkshire (me, a gaping, gleeful, eight-year-old passenger beside her); as she licked from her lips the residue of some oozing cream-cake (a sweet tooth which only slowly taxed her figure); as she held up to herself, like some flimsy, snatched-up dancing partner, a newly bought frock: 'Divine, darling! Isn't it just *divine*!'

I cannot summon my father so easily. I have no touchstone. Perhaps because of what happened. Perhaps because, in any case

Photo: The Hulton Picture Company

(sons need time—they truly need time—to get to know their fathers), he was always a distant and sombre figure, outshone, first to his delight, then to his consternation, by my mother's heedless brightness. Yet I remember him once attempting to draw near—or so I think that was his intention. It was in that same Paris apartment, on a cold, windy evening, with winter still at war with spring, the lights on outside and a fire burning hearteningly in the massive, grey marble fireplace. He was standing by the fire, one elbow on the mantelpiece, in full evening rig, waiting for my mother before they left for another of his official functions.

'The thing is,' he suddenly said, slowly, with an air of weighed wisdom and of speaking aloud some uncontainable thought, 'when you are out on an adventure, you want to be at home by the fire, and when you are at home by the fire, you want to be out on an adventure.'

I wish I knew what it was I had said—if anything—that elicited that unusual pithiness. And I wish I had known then, while the fire flickered and the wind scraped at the windows, what should have been the proper response. I was nine. There he was, in all his pride, fifty-five years old—more than twenty years older than my mother; medals on chest, cigar lit, scotch and soda—a large one—poured. Some question of mine? Or some impulse in his own mind that seemed to raise the whole, daunting phenomenon of his soldierly past and his mysterious present duties, his aura of belonging to a world of great, glorious (but peculiarly awkward) things?

He seemed surprised, himself, at his own words, as if he had not known they were stored inside him. He looked self-consciously at his watch.

'Whatever can your mother be up to?'

Perhaps it was on that same evening—but this surely would have been sooner after our arrival—that I had asked him, point-blank, what were we doing, what was *he* doing, here in Paris? And he'd replied, with a sort of jocular, self-effacing gravity, 'Oh—sorting out the world. You know, that sort of thing.'

Only once can I remember his attempting to show me the sights of Paris. We had scarcely set out—our first port of call was Napoleon's tomb—when an icy shower caught us, the first of a series which would turn our jaunt into a stoical exercise. I could not help feeling how I would much rather have been with my mother. How she would have turned a change in the weather into a positive pleasure: wrestling, laughing, with an umbrella; scurrying into the aromatic warmth of a café and ordering, in an Anglo-French that was infinitely more convincing if no more proficient than his, '*Un crême, un jus d'orange*,' and, falling back into expressive English, 'and two of those wicked little tarts!'

Seeing the sights of Paris with my mother! Shopping sprees with my mother in Paris! From her I learnt to see the world as a scintillating shop window, a confection, a display of tempting frippery. From her I learnt the delights of ogling and coveting and—by proxy and complicity—spending. I would go with her to spend money. To buy hats, necklaces, gloves, shoes, dresses, cakes. I would wait, perched on a velvet-backed chair, smiled at by the attentive *vendeuse*, while, behind drawn plush curtains, things slithered, rustled, snapped to an accompaniment of sighs and hums. In the city of perfume we bought perfume. In the city of lingerie we pondered over lascivious creations of silk and lace. If they were meant expressly for his eyes, it only made his noble loftiness the more impressive; but I suspected—I knew—they were not. And in all this I was the adjudicator, the referee, the scapegoat. The oyster-grey or the rose-pink? 'Oh, you decide, sweetie. No, you can't? *Bien, tous les deux, s'il vous plaît, Madame*.'

'*Tous les deux, Madame? Ah oui, d'accord. Le petit est bon juge, n'est-ce pas?*'

Coming out with her booty, she would hug me ardently, as if it were I who had enabled her so successfully to succumb. In the same way, prior to such purchases, when her eyes fell on anything particularly delicious and desirable in a window, she would squeeze me fiercely, conspiratorially, giving an Ooh! or an Aah! as if it were I alone who could tilt the balance between mere looking and rushing headlong into the shop. 'But isn't it just *heavenly*, darling?' I could have lived for, lived in that squeeze. Until I grew up and realized it was almost entirely selfish. She might as well have been hugging herself, or a handy cushion or a spaniel.

Sorting out the world! He should have sorted out himself and his own jeopardized household. Did he know—but he must have done from the very beginning, he must have known what she was 'up to'—that while he was busy sorting out the world and 'talking with the Allies' (another cryptic phrase, which made me think of some gossipy, over-neighbourly family) and I was busy at the little *école* for foreigners they found for me, '*Maman*', as I'd begun precociously to call her, was busy entertaining or being entertained by Uncle Sam, or plain Sam Ellison as he then was, who had his own recipe for sorting out the world, expressible in one single, vulgar word: plastics. In *Maman*'s defence, it could be said that she too was engaged with the Allies, Sam being American. And in Sam's defence, it could be said that, fuelled as it was by rank commercialism, he too had a sense of mission.

'It's the stuff that's gonna mould the future. I mean, literally. Anything from a coffee cup to an artificial leg, to the sock that goes on it.'

'And then there's plastic surgery.'

'No, that's kinda different, sweetheart.'

(As my mother, an expert at lash-fluttering *fausse-naïveté*, well knew.)

He must have known. If I could sniff these matters out, even in their early, covert stages, then he—. But then I was a virtual accomplice. When I emerged from my *école* in the afternoon to see Sam just dropping *Maman* off from a taxi, or made my own way home to find her in a distinct state of having hastily bathed and dressed, I would receive not guilty looks but one of her swift, smothering, implicating hugs—essentially no different from her shopping hugs. Thank you for letting me buy that dress—isn't it gorgeous? Thank you for letting me fuck Sam—isn't he di-vine? And, yes, that word had only to spring from her lips and I believed it to be so. I thought Sam—six feet of hard-muscled American avarice—was divine, and I thought *crêpe suzette* and *tarte tatin* were divine, and I thought oyster-grey silk cami-knickers were divine, and I thought my mother's laughter, the sheer, vicious gaiety in her eyes, was divine.

'Do up my buttons, sweetie, would you? There's an angel.'

A whole world existed in which men did up the backs of women's dresses at four o'clock in the afternoon.

And what world was he sorting out? Some new, rebuilt world which would one day be unveiled to the dazzlement and shame of such backsliders as Mother and me? Or some old, dream-world restored, in which implacable British sergeant-majors bawled for ever over far-flung parade grounds and men followed well-trodden paths to glory and knighthoods?

He was fifty-five. And I had the insight of an infant. But it seems, now, that I could have told him then: that world was gone. An axe had dropped on it.

Paris. April in Paris. Paris was nonetheless still Paris. I had never seen Paris before, and yet even at nine years old I had this recurring sensation of encountering a vision made fact. If the *trompe-l'oeil* Paris of *La Bohème* was an illusion, then on my journeys on foot between our apartment and the *école*, journeys which took a meandering form and had something to do, I suppose now, with a sense of having lost the right path with my parents, I daily disproved the illusion: Paris was the living, breathing rendition of itself.

Somewhere on those wanderings to and from school, in the crisp, rimy breath of a January morning, I looked up from the pavement through a tall, lighted window and saw—a true vision. Three—four, five—ballerinas, dressed in leotards and tights, swathed in woollen leg-warmers, dipping, stretching, balancing, raising one leg, extending one arm in that curving way ballet-dancers do, while clinging with the other to a wall-bar. I stood transfixed, entranced. How many times did I pass that window again? How many times was the blind cruelly drawn? Once—but this must have been at a later time of day and I must have been by then a fully-fledged truant, *flâneur*, *voyeur*—I passed a café at the further end of the same street, and there, sitting at an outside table, even in that midwinter chill (warm and pink from exercise) were my ballerinas. But no longer poised, living sculptures. They were little chattering *mesdemoiselles*-about-town, crossing their legs, nestling their chins into their scarves, responding boldly to the *badinage* of the waiter, blowing at the steamy froth on their *chocolats chauds.* I drew close, feigning interest in an adjacent shop-front. Glowing faces. A sound of female glee. Two eyes, in particular, beneath a dark fringe, which momentarily turned on me. Two pink lips, a flicking tongue adorned with the flakes of a croissant.

A crude case of my mother's shop-window lusts? But I knew it was more than that. What enthralled me was the pathos, the dignity, the ardour of *rehearsal.* The sublime fact that in a world so in need of being sorted out, young girls of sixteen and seventeen (but, of course, to me, then, they were Women) could devote themselves so strenuously to becoming sugar-plum fairies.

Lift the axe! I wish I could have taken him, gripped his hand, as he gripped mine, suddenly, on that wet, chilly day as we emerged from the gloom of *Les Invalides*, stood him before that secret window, and said: There, it's for that that you are sorting out the world. I wish he could have gripped my hand more firmly still, come closer to me out of his remoteness; told me, warned me.

Paris first bred in me the notion that the highest aim of civilization is the loving perfection of the useless: ballerinas, café chatter, Puccini operas, Elizabethan sonnets, silk underwear, *parfumerie*, *patisserie*, chandeliers, the magic hush when the lights go down in an auditorium . . .

'*Mimi! Mimi! Mimi!*'

. . . and Romantic Love.

She actually cried, she actually wept in the seat beside me, dabbing her eyes and clutching my hand, while her lips mimed the arias.

Lift the axe! A Paris morning, in April. Perhaps that very morning I had peeped at my ballerinas. Morning turning to midday. Sunshine; pigeons; the smell of food. She is waiting beyond the gates of the *école*, though by now I am used to making my own way home. She is alone and somehow purposeful, fixed in her own space. She opens her arms and gives me an engulfing hug, as if I have returned from somewhere far away. But she is not smiling (or crying). She is composed and authoritative; the hug is like some solemn ceremony.

'Your Daddy has had an accident, at his office.'

'An accident?'

'Your Daddy has had an accident. And died.'

The second part of this statement, uttered unemphatically, almost perfunctorily, scarcely registered at first. Certain announcements take time to reach the brain.

'An accident with a gun.'

With a gun? With a *gun*? What was he doing, in his office, in Paris, in the seventh *arrondissement*, in the centre of civilization, with a gun? A sudden, racing fantasy, a whole alternative life for my father, who was now dead, bloomed in my head. He was a spy, an undercover agent, he was on some hush-hush mission. It explained his distance, his absences, his resonant words about 'adventure'. He bore the constant burden of secrecy and danger. For a while the delusion was so strong that it turned into a pang of regret: I had discovered this source of excitement too late—I could never, now, have access to it.

And perhaps it was this sense of deprivation rather than the simple fact that my father was dead, that made tears rush to my eyes.

'Yes, my darling, you cry. Cry. Cry.'

And, opening her arms again, stooping, but unweeping, she crushed me against that warm, ready bosom, where Sam, by now, must already have been crushed many times.

She never used the word 'suicide'. Perhaps I would not have known what it meant. Perhaps I guessed and only wanted, as she did, to gloss over the fact. It was Sam, in any case, who confirmed my suspicions. He and I were alone in the apartment. She had become a busy woman. I knew nothing about inquest proceedings, let alone in foreign cities. This must have been before she and I went back, the first time, with the body, to Berkshire.

I said, 'He meant to do it, didn't he?'

A bold, grown-up, not-to-be-evaded question.

'Yes, pal. I guess so.'

Later, it occurred to me that Sam might have been briefed to deal with this very point. But his brief, or his aptitude for it, only went so far. I was nine, he was twenty-four. Twenty-four seems now such a slender age—not so far from nine—but there was no doubt that during that time in Paris those fifteen years between Sam and me could be a wide gap to leap. Not so wide, it's true, as the forty-six years between me and my father. Which gave Sam a distinct advantage in winning me over—along with the ability to slide into a boyish, big-brotherly familiarity quite beyond my father. But I always thought this was just a knack, an act for my benefit.

That morning, days after my father's death, was the first time that it occurred to me, from the vantage of my own unlooked-for access of experience, that Sam really was, perhaps, just a kid. The fact that almost as big a gap of years existed between him and my mother as between him and me did not escape me. Once, on one of those tumultuous afternoons that seemed now to belong to another age, I had heard my mother simper, beyond closed, impassive doors, 'Come on Sammy, come to Mummy . . .' I recalled it now, not recognizing one of the least exceptional tropes of love. It was as though at the very point when Sam was most culpable, I both saw he was most innocent and discovered a new cause for enmity.

He took out a cigarette and I saw that his hand, his strong, young man's hand, was shaking. He must have known I'd seen it.

'Why?' I said. The inevitable follow-up.

But 'why' was not one of Sam's words, the scrutiny of motives was not his strong point.

'I guess you'll have to ask your mother that, pal.' He managed to light the cigarette and took a deep, steadying draw.

'I guess I'll have to be looking after your mother now,' he added with a kind of feeble cheerfulness, as if the statement were half a question; as if he were watching his youth melt away.

I asked my mother. She was ready to be asked. I suppose there must have been some confabulation between them, a two-stage strategy. It was the moment, of course, for her to have broken down, wept, begged my forgiveness, confessed that her shamelessness had driven a man to his death. The things that happen in opera, they happen in life too. But she didn't. She spoke calmly, almost dreamily.

'Perhaps there was something he knew that we shall never know.'

Which was, of course, a twisting round of the truth. It was we who had known something which he hadn't known; or which he had known all along and could no longer pretend not to know. Her eyes hardened into a sort of warning whose meaning was clear: Don't play the innocent, sweetie. If I'm to blame, then so are you. You were a party to this. You allowed it, didn't you? You let it happen.

It was true: I might have gone to him at any time, like a true, a dutiful, a worthy son. Spilled the beans.

Then suddenly she smiled tenderly and took me in her arms. 'Poor darling,' she said, as if I had fallen and grazed my knee. As if at the same time she thought this whole line of thinking were unnecessarily morbid. We were alive; my father was dead. She had taken Sam into her life. She had known what she was doing; she had made her choice. The fierceness, the frankness of her will to live! She told me, many years later, with complete equanimity, how she had gone to see him in the mortuary. How his head was swathed in bandages, save his face. How they had even put a sticking-plaster over the hole in his temple. She had no squeamishness. No pity, no mercy. I think she even despised him for his death, which, for all its drastic convenience, was nonetheless cowardly, stupid, messy, extreme. She despised this man she had married, exploited, cheated—destroyed.

And it was true. If I had an allegiance, it was to her, not to him. The image of my father rose before me, as inscrutable, as open to interpretation as it was deserving of belated loyalty. He must have known for weeks about the two of them. And even if the penny had dropped only late in the day, did suicide truly answer the circumstances? A former soldier, a man of action. If a bullet was to be involved, it should surely have been placed neatly between Sam Ellison's eyes.

A recurring dream—the very emblem of my addled adolescence: Sam with a fresh, damson-coloured hole (and no sticking plaster) in his forehead.

But perhaps Sam and Mother were only the last, ill-timed straw. I underestimated the dimensions of the man, who was no more. During those strange, transitional months, as we moved from Paris back to Berkshire, as Mother married Sam and I reached my tenth birthday, the awesome realization offered itself to me that my father had tried but had simply not been able to sort out the world. People die when their world will no longer sustain them. Duty, ambition, prestige and even, now, his wife had let him down. He was fifty-five years old. I can see him feeling the cool weight of the pistol. The 'honourable way out'; a soldier's solution. When you are out on an adventure . . . Suddenly death, not the vivid, vaunted death of the battlefield, but the image of himself as a duped nonentity stared him in the face—and he rushed to meet it.

Lift the axe! Put the pistol back! Carry me back to that world of boulevards and ballerinas. To that songful, mirthful, deceitful apartment. Carry me back even to the innocence of that moment of icy, naked shock—I had never felt it before—round which my mother, by the *école* gates, cast her cloaking embrace. There was a space in the world occupied by my father which would never be occupied by him again. The spring sun falling on Parisian shutters, Parisian cobbles, was gentle, kindly, beyond reproach. It fell on the fur collar of my mother's coat and picked out of its filaments little pin-points of gold. All that day I seemed to see that the sunshine was made up of countless particles of irreducible, indestructible, eternal gold.

2

I was born in December, 1936, in the very week that a King of England gave up his crown in order to marry the woman he loved. Naturally, I knew nothing about this at the time and, of course, other events than the Abdication Crisis were then at large in the world. But I have always felt that the timing of my arrival imbued my life, for better or worse, with a sort of fairy-tale propensity. I have always had a soft spot (a naïve view, I know) for the throneless ex-King sitting it out on the Riviera. And I have often wondered whether my mother's pangs with me on that December day were eased by that concurrent event which must have been viewed by many, rather than as a crisis, as a welcome intrusion of Romance, allowing them fondly to forget for a moment Hitler, Mussolini and Franco. All for Love. Or, The World Well Lost. 'Let . . . the wide arch of the ranged empire fall!' (As indeed it began to do under poor, put-upon George VI.) All for love, yes. *Amor vincit* . . .

And Paris, fairy-tale city, might have endorsed the point. Paris, with its enchanted streets and eternal air of licensed felicity might have taken me to its heart. Was there any other city in the world in which to live but Paris? I might have become one of those countless aspirants who have flocked to the city by the Seine and become great artists, great dreamers or great liars. I might have become, trained in the free school of my mother and Sam, a great *boulevardier*, a great philanderer. I might have lived the life of Reilly. But my father died before I had even passed the gates of puberty. And what I became was—bookish.

Though this did not happen immediately. If the truth be known, when we returned to England I didn't grieve for my dead father. I didn't want to grieve for him. I didn't want to think of him. I didn't want to think of my father as the man who had fired a gun at his head. I grieved for my adorable ballet-girls, who by this stage had received honorary names—delicious, seductive French names—Yvette, Simone, Michelle—who, even then, were alive and literally kicking, stretching their beautiful limbs in the ballet school, utterly ignorant of my distant worship and entirely without need of it.

And this was not a good time for grief. Or rather, it was a very good time for grief, which made one little parcel of it unexceptional and negligible. People had got used in recent times to the fact that every so often, so it seemed, nature required a culling, and thus to mixing a little callousness with their sorrow. Perhaps it was only after my father's demise that the war, which I had lived through but conceived of as some remote, rumbling, impenetrably grown-up affair, became real for me. It was about death; slaughter, bodies, casualty lists.

And if I did not grasp the general point, I had the specific reminder of Ed. Shot down, aged nineteen-and-a-half, over the blue Pacific. A photo of his grinning brother became Sam's trump card. How could I take out my feelings on Sam, how could I unleash on him all the venom due an arrant usurper (a murderer in all but name), when he neatly reminded me that we were companions in the same grim business of bereavement?

And what was an 'accident' with a pistol in a Paris office to the Battle of the Coral Sea? ('Yep, a lot of brave boys went down . . .'—his sentence would end in a mimetic gulp.) And what was my father's death to the deaths of the fathers of other boys (I met them, these high-grade orphans) who had died, as the saying went, 'in action'? My father, soldier though he was, had died in circumstances which required from me either a considerable degree of risky inventiveness or a suspect, rumour-breeding silence.

And how could I deny—for all his exploitation of it—Sam's plight? You are twenty-one years old, happily exempted, for complex reasons of primogeniture and your father's involvement in a new and militarily useful industry ('Perspex, pal—you heard about perspex?') from armed service. But your younger brother, your little kid brother, Ed, joins up, learns to fly and is killed. It might have been you, you think: it should have been you. Whatever you do now will be over your brother's dead, sea-shrouded body. You have to live for Ed now; to take on all Ed's lost chances (and Ed was great with the girls, they just fell over him). To become a perpetual nineteen-year-old.

'Sure—it's tough. I know. It hits you hard,' was the extent of his attempts to sound out the measure of my sorrow and show his willingness, if necessary, to console. I have to admit he handled with a degree of delicacy the problem of disguising his relief that I didn't appear to be hopelessly distraught, while preparing for the onset of a possibly vicious delayed reaction. And there was, in any case, that air of frank confidingness (so unlike my father), that bluff disavowal—I'm sorry if I have no conscience, if I have no shame, but it's not my fault—that thick-skinned, businessman's charm.

But I knew just how thick-skinned he really was. I had seen him with his hand trembling—I would see him, twice again in my life, with his face as drained of vigour as it was on that day. I knew his weakness. His tactical strength was his strategic disadvantage. Even I could see that, with all its fraught implications, with all its dangerous blend of the expedient and the needful, Sam saw in me a bizarre substitute for Ed. (And you gotta have substitutes.) That he side-stepped the dread question of his surrogate paternity—not to say his entire adult responsibilities—by this appeal to the chummily fraternal.

And he was right to prepare for a delayed reaction. He underestimated, that's all, the extent of the delay and the persistence of the reaction. It seems that I'm a slow burner, a long-term investor of emotions.

We returned, briefly, to Berkshire in April 1946, to follow my father's coffin, then permanently in June to settle in his home. I had a strong sense now of its being 'my father's house' rather than 'home', though my mother rapidly began asserting her proprietorial rights. Furniture was replaced. Decorators appeared. There was plainly money on tap. The little gallery of framed photographs from above the sideboard, recording the 'India days' (cane chairs; verandahs; turbans; polo sticks) disappeared one morning in the van of a man collecting for a jumble sale. I did not believe, any more than my mother, that the place should become a shrine to her husband's memory, but I felt the injustice. And I felt, as the physical remnants of my father were whittled away, the accretion, as it were, of his ghostly stock. It was *his* house. He may not have earned his plot in the ethereal fields of fame but he had left this solid enough memorial. It was the husk of his life.

I should have protested. I should have said, at least, about those photographs: take them from the dining-room, if you will, but let me keep them in my bedroom. But the hypocrite and the coward in me stopped my tongue.

They got married the following March. There was a decent interval in which she practised being a widow and Sam, to give him his credit, kept his relative distance, turning up only for plainly licentious weekends. It's true, he had much to occupy him. He was sowing (also) the seeds of his little empire—spreading the bright, new gospel of polymers. I still have a vision of him offering his New World marvels to a depressed and war-wrecked England. The picture merges with all those smiling GIs, in their jaunty jeeps, handing out gum and being kissed and garlanded in the ruins of liberated villages. This was not Sam's experience, but he was built in the appropriate mould, and perhaps even imagined himself in the same blithely triumphal role.

Unlike many of his countrymen hustling their way round Europe in those days, Sam did not simply have a suitcase full of nylons, he had a father in Cleveland with a factory that *made* nylons, and young as he was, a sound working knowledge of industrial chemistry. Above all, he had an inborn flair for business. I think of Sam as a perpetual juvenile in all other respects, but in business he had powers beyond his years.

Of the origin of the flair, of Sam's parentage, of 'old man Ellison', clearly one of America's leading plastics pioneers, I know very little; only that he and Sam had had a falling out, the roots of which seemed to have been the old man's egotism and Ed's death. There was Ellison senior, the self-made tycoon, and there was Ed at the bottom of the ocean. And in between the two was Sam, the dutiful, filial protégé, the safe, underwritten, overshadowed, guilt-ridden schmuck. Sam had to go his own way, or become the eternal stooge. The necessary scenes of confrontation and rebellion should have prepared him, you might think, for my own act of rebellion in flatly refusing (I could see it coming a mile off) his own bountiful offer of a life in plastic. He might have been mercifully inclined, even nostalgically respectful. Not a bit of it. There was not even what I took to be old Ellison's final compromise: a sizeable pay-off and the injunction to get lost and get rich.

Like father, like son. I wonder. In going his own way, you could say Sam only did in reverse what his own father had done some decades before when he upped sticks and crossed the promise-laden Atlantic. Sam pitched his hopes in the opposite direction, in an old continent which history had nonetheless turned into a new wilderness where opportunities abounded for the bold and the resourceful, and where it was still possible, in such callings as plastics, to be a pioneer. Thus he partook of that post-war spirit of inverse colonialism which beguiled and affronted the exhausted folk of the old world—yet which, in Sam's case, was to be reversed yet again, to melt in that grotesque dream of actual assimilation, actual assumption into the true, old world.

But the release from paternal oppression also gave the perpetual kid-at-heart within Sam its liberty. Thus it was that, with a view to a little holiday, a little sight-seeing before the serious business of life began (and with Ed's robbed youth as well as his own to think of), Sam came to Paris.

It seems to me now that, but for my father's extreme action, my mother might have been for Sam only a ship that passed in the night. He was too soft-centred a soul simply to run away from the mess, and he found himself caught. But this is only one interpretation, and it begs the question of who was the predator and who (or what) was the prey. There was the factor of my mother's (i.e. my father's) money, which would indubitably have come in handy for a young man pledged to an independent life, let alone to setting up his own business. However big the cut he received from old Ellison, Sam must have been running through it fast enough in Paris. My father died; Sam saw his opportunity. It would, of course, be interesting to know whether he saw his opportunity *before* my father died.

Then there was the factor (I cannot overlook this—I heard the squeals from the bedroom) of sheer carnal compulsion. They hit it off. I have to say it. Sam brought to a melting ripeness the full fruits of my mother's womanhood, poorly tended as perhaps they were by my father. Perhaps because of his obligation to function for two, Sam was on some sort of biological overdrive. But—I have to say this too—my mother could give as good as she took. And in all this she was not blind. Sam was the blind one, at least when his eyes (I only quote an expression he once used, with rare self-appraisal, of himself) were only in his balls. I think she took stock of her precarious seniority. She gave herself an interval of fleshly fulfilment, during which time she would set Sam up (the question still stands: how much was Ellison Plastics my mother's work?), and thus enjoy, in her mellower years, with a little diplomatic flexibility (the biological overdrive was an ongoing thing), both the rewards and the control.

An image of Sam, indelible in the memory, from one of those weekends during our first months back in England. A sultry summer's night; I get up to fetch a glass of water: Sam on the landing, stark naked, caught between bedroom and bathroom, and in a state of livid tumescence. He drops a hand in almost maidenly alarm. He says, 'Oh hi, Paul,' with a kind of strangulated nonchalance, as if we have met on some street corner. Never thereafter is the encounter mentioned by either of us.

Only when the image of my ballet-girls faded did grief for my father emerge to take its place. Or rather, not grief itself but a nagging, self-pitying, self-accusatory emotion born of the guilt at not feeling grief (how could I sigh over young sylphs in tutus when my own father was dead?) and out of a mood of redundancy, which it occurred to me my father must have felt too. There were Sam and my mother testing the springs of a new double bed, and there was I, an adjunct, an accessory, a supernumerary. This had been my father's position. I stood in his vacant place. And out of this ghostly identification I began to summon a father I had never really known: noble, virtuous, wronged.

I'd like to think I wasn't as slow as I was in opening my account of vengeance; that at least by that day the India photos were removed, I had taken my first vow of retribution; and that if I took such a vow, it was as authentic and spontaneous as the pang that prompted it. But I'm not so sure. I'm not so sure if our passions seek out models of behaviour or if models of behaviour are the springs of our passions. It was a while before the first blow was struck.

When I was eleven I went to a new school. I expected to excel in French. Instead, I excelled in English; I took comfort in books. I'd like to think that the love of literature which fell into my life around this time was a pure and genuine love, lighting my darkened and orphaned days. But I cannot be sure. I cannot be sure which came first: the love of literature which ensured I would cherish the play; or the play, which guaranteed I would venerate literature. In any case, my English master was called Tubby Baxter, a thin and cadaverous man, naturally, having the air now and then of a haunted and death-obsessed Renaissance hero. And the play, as you may have guessed, was *Hamlet*.

So what should I have done? Drawn my poniard and stabbed his unguarded back? 'Now might I do it pat . . .'

What I actually did was this. . .

Sam believed in gifts. He persistently showered them on me, not merely on birthdays and special occasions—gifts that were so transparently aimed at winning my filial allegiance that it was a simple matter to rebuff him with formal gratitude and immediate neglect of the article in question. These gifts tended to have a masculine and practical as well as an American bias. So I received a 'Walt Disney Super Annual' as well as a chemistry set and the inevitable trains (but here he hit a genuine soft spot and nearly weakened resolve: before there were ballet-dancers, you see, there were trains).

One day I was handed a gift that, even in this tiresome succession of bribes, I appreciated was special. It was a model aircraft kit. That is, a *plastic*, scale-model aircraft kit of a type soon to flood the British market. This, however, was a kit of American origin in a large, spectacular box. Inside the box—somewhat belying its lavish dimensions—were fuselage and wing parts and, attached to thin strips from which they could be snapped off, a host of intricately detailed smaller fixtures: propellor, wing flaps, undercarriage and so on—even, complete with moulded flying-jacket and helmet, a little, rigidly alert pilot.

I wish I could remember the name of the plane. I ought to. It was a rather stocky-looking fighter plane, once in service with the US Navy. But what I remember is the box and the almost cinemascope vividness of the scene emblazoned on its lid. We are high in the air, amidst a tight, attacking formation of the nameless aircraft, one of which is caught in fine close-up—diving angle, guns ablaze—at centre-picture. Below us is the blue sheen of the Pacific, and on it the Japanese fleet taking frantic evasive action: flashing guns, smoke, curving wakes. In the distance, a skirmish between our planes and their defending fighters, one of which, gashed with flame, spirals towards the sea.

The compound symbolism of this offering was not lost on a boy capable of reading and digesting *Hamlet*.

'You see what you can do with plastic, pal? This is a *scale*-model. Everything's an exact replica of the real thing . . .' He went on, as if he were talking not about plastic but about some kind of protoplasm.

And I did not have to ask, though I did ask, with an ingenuous and reverend hesitancy, and received from Sam a dry-voiced reply and a melting look, as if we were on the verge of a breakthrough: 'Was this the plane that Ed . . .?'

We spread the pieces on the table. He interpreted the little leaflet of instructions. His face, with its clean, naïve features that would age so well (how did this man ever succeed in business?) hung close to mine. It was obvious that he was having to restrain himself from assembling the model himself.

'Well, kid—all yours. Make a good job of it.'

And make a good job of it I did. How I pleased him by not rejecting this bribe but giving it my devoted attention. What pains I took to assemble each piece in the correct order and not to smear the glue. And this diligence had its strangely revelatory side. Under my hands, something came to life: a piece of history, a fragment of former time viewed down the wrong end of a telescope. When I fitted the little pilot into his cockpit—duly painted in advance: pink for the face, brown for his leather jacket—I felt that I was like the hand of fate itself. I could see very clearly an inexorable truth. The man thought he was in control of the plane but it was the plane that was in control of the man. This was how things stood. The man didn't belong to himself. The man was plucked up from his real place and set down in the plane no less ruthlessly than I took his miniature counterpart and glued him down by his backside. The man was a fleshy anomaly, entirely at the mercy of his winged carapace. He might as well have been made of plastic.

When the plane was assembled, fastidiously painted in authentic camouflage and affixed with its marking transfers, I hung it by a length of thread from the ceiling in my bedroom.

This seemed both an appropriate aerial perch and to suggest the status of a treasured icon—I would look at it last thing at night and first thing in the morning.

But it didn't remain there for long.

The following morning, in fact, a warm Sunday morning, I took it down. Below me, on the paved terrace at the rear of the house, overlooked by my bedroom, Sam and my mother were lounging in deck-chairs, a late breakfast over. There was, I remember, a peculiar calm about this Sunday morning—the rustle of papers, the clink of coffee cups—a feeling of probation served, as if we had reached a pitch of domestic equilibrium not yet achieved.

I held the lovingly constructed aircraft in one hand and with the other applied a lighted match to the propellor. Plastic, as Sam liked to drive home, does not oxidize or decompose and is resistant to electricity; but it is not un-inflammable. It burns with a spluttering, tenacious flame and a thick, black smoke, reminiscent of burning oil. Thus a plastic plane can be destroyed as well as built with a good deal of verisimilitude.

The propellor, then the engine cowling ignited, filling my bedroom with evil fumes of which Sam and my mother had so far no inkling. Holding the plane with the bold patience of a grenade thrower, I waited till the flames—the propellor already a bubbling goo—began to lick the cockpit and the little trapped pilot. Then, standing before the open window and throwing back my arm, I hurled it up and out, so that it soared first high over the heads of Sam and my mother, then plummeted downwards, with a remarkably realistic smoke-trailing effect, to crash just a few feet in front of them on the lawn, one wing dislodged, but still ablaze.

I went to the window—partly because it was my intention to be brazen, partly in order to gasp for air. I heard my mother's startled 'Good God!'; Sam's 'What the—?!' They both leapt from their seats. My mother tried to beat out the fire with a hastily folded *News of the World*, while Sam, telling her to get out the way, took the lid from the coffee pot and emptied its contents over the wreckage. Only then did they look up. My mother was a picture of exasperated accusation, as if I had simply spoilt a promising day, but Sam was already entering the house in an unprecedented rage. I sat calmly on my bed. He appeared in the doorway, and checked himself momentarily—either because my composure unnerved him or because of the fog of smoke filling the room. As he paused I had time to see—through the murk—that though his face was twisted with anger, it was also blanched with horror. It was the look of a man whose direct thoughts, whose worst fears have been exposed.

'You little son of a bitch!' he yelled. 'You little goddam son of a bitch!'

The window was open and my mother must have heard. And I wonder now how much Sam supposed he was uttering the truth.

GRANTA

NOTES FROM ABROAD

Cairo
David Grossman

I had read dozens of articles about Cairo, yet to describe this city properly, newsprint would have to become hunched, wrinkled, odoriferous, screeching, perspiring, and able to envelop you in a mist of sweat and smoke. Cairo empties you instantly, leaving only eyes and ears and nose. Before I came to Cairo I had never understood what a crowd is, or how many cars you could see at once, stuck to each other, then suddenly breaking free and charging off wildly, each car grazing the one in front of it, people jumping out from under wheels at the last possible second, clusters of people hanging on to the outside of ancient buses, and all the time, during the day and at night, horns blaring warnings and winks and curses and apologies and, Look out, friend, here I come from the far left-hand lane, I'm taking a right angle over three lanes, I'm swerving around a woman who has put down her year-old baby in the middle of the road and bent down to put his even smaller brother on her shoulders, and excuse me air-conditioned Mercedes with your tight-lipped Kuwaiti driver staring in front at three humble donkeys harnessed to a wagon overflowing with garbage on top of which five-year-old children are sleeping peacefully.

It becomes clear that the only way to get out of the *zahama*, the traffic jam, is to do what my driver does and cross the solid line when there's a red light, and then drive the wrong way, past thousands of stuck cars to a policeman at a crossroads, his uniform gleaming white from a distance on a morning as good as the skin on your milk, and warmly shake the policeman's hand while at the same time pressing half an Egyptian lira into his palm, and suddenly you've broken free and escaped the jam, you're driving rampant against the traffic and no one tries to block you, no one interferes, they assume that if a person drives that way, he has a reason. Anyway, by then you're already approaching the next junction, and the next bank-note is ready in your palm: one of those creased, sweat-soaked Egyptian bills that are exchanged hundreds of times each day, until their texture becomes like that of a labourer's hands.

I am astonished. How can it be that tens of thousands and millions of antiquated cars screech through this city, without signs, without signalling, without cursing, with no help but the complex code of horns, and there are almost no accidents? When a car did crash into us, I felt almost relieved. A strange spell had been broken. It turned out that the driver was Israeli. Oh well, let's look the other way and quickly tell about the myriad policemen and soldiers dressed in torn uniforms and thongs, uselessly guarding every square and intersection. The sternness their position requires is alien to their whole selves: they aim their rifles aimlessly, getting through another watch and as the time passes, thoughts like amber prayer beads slowly roll through their heads. The mosques call out Allah and the people say Allah, over and over, at every moment, from every direction, *Allahu akbar*, *elemarallah*, *inshallah*, like an incessant drip, or the clopping of the surprisingly soft feet of camels on the asphalt.

But stop. Step aside from the crowd a minute and look: because, after all, these are the same people who, twenty-three years ago, gulped down the bloody speeches of Gamel Abd el-Nasser and marched through these very streets, crazed with hatred for my country. And what is the most astonishing thing about them? Their serenity, the way in which they avoid any gesture of violence or vulgarity.

'Take the Holocaust, for instance,' says Salwah Gamgum, a well-known Egyptian journalist. 'I was in Israel and visited that horrible place, Yad Vashem. Why must you return to the Holocaust all the time?'.

I am asked about the Holocaust in almost every

conversation I have in Egypt. Attorney Abd el-Jaffer Rizkanah, and Hassan Ali, a Voice of Cairo newscaster, and Yehieh Sa'ad and Nur Mahmad and Tarek el-Marshawi, students of the Hebrew language at Cairo university, ask: 'Why do all the books you write dredge up that horrible event? After all, your history has good, pleasant periods in it, too. For instance when you were in the Arab countries and were protected by Islam. Why don't you write about that?'

I count to ten. I hold myself back. I came here to listen.

'The Holocaust makes you think that everyone hates you. It makes you hard, bitter.' The three Hebrew-speaking students are trying to help me understand. Their faces are sincere, concerned; they are explaining something that is manifestly clear to them: 'Here, we had wars with you, and now we've made peace—everything is already forgotten. We've forgotten. Why dig into your soul and be tortured?'

I look for some hint in their faces of their real, hidden, hostile intention. They can't really believe that a nation should—or can—uproot itself from its past and erase its scars?

'We in Egypt have no consciousness of the Holocaust,' says Tahsin Rashir, formerly President Mubarak's personal ambassador, a dark-faced man with an ancient gaze. 'At most we see it as the way in which you justify your treatment of Arabs, and then, clearly, we have little patience for it. We have no knowledge of what is being written in Hebrew—especially about the Holocaust. There is no translation of Anne Frank into Arabic. How can we understand you? The Egyptians are not trying, God forbid, to minimize the importance of the Holocaust or its horror.'

I listen to him. I refrain from making arguments about the sympathy many Egyptians, including Sadat, had for the Nazis. I came here to listen.

'You do not know how to love,' says A.H., a public official relieved of his job because, he says, of his overly favourable attitude to Israel (this is why he asks to remain anonymous). 'You do not know how to be good friends. You are even afraid to love a woman with all your heart, in case she betrays you.'

I look at him: 'We don't know what friendship is? *We* don't?'

'You are people full of fear and anger and violence. Your past made you that way. Now you just fight all the time—in business, in your scientific research and in your relations with other people.'

'And you? What can you tell me about the Egyptians?'

'With us it is different. We live at an entirely different pace. Very slow. We can devote time to friendship. We are people who know how to live in one place. You are fighters. We know how to love.' A chuckle sends his mouth askew. 'Perhaps because of that you will always win. You won the wars. You have also won the peace.'

'We won the peace? The peace is our victory? You didn't get anything from it?'

'We're losers. Look: you won peace with a very large and strong enemy. You received oil at ridiculous prices. In exchange, you gave us the Sinai. We already had plenty of desert.'

I gaze at him in astonishment, thinking about all the Israelis who feel the magnitude of the sacrifice we made when we gave up the security of the Sinai. What is there between the Egyptian and the Israeli people? Why do we insist on flaunting our own wounds, but do not dare feel each other's pain? How did our strength fail us a few steps before the peak, after such huge efforts were invested?

In an alley we come face to face with a car coming in the wrong direction. We exchange a few honks, and wait. My driver—a muscular man with a stern expression—shrugs. The man facing us honks again. Three, four, ten minutes pass, and cars pile up behind both of us. At this point, in Israel, the drivers would be at each other's throats, rolling in the dirt of the pavement. Here, no one moves. The drivers don't even look at each other. Slowly passers-by and idlers gather to watch what is happening. But no one seems to want a fight. On the contrary there seems to be apprehension and unease that there will be a confrontation. The two drivers sit motionless in their cars. Both of them seem perplexed and distressed—their shoulders hang low—as if they have been tricked by fate into this predicament. For heaven's sake, I think, when, finally, a sort of compromise is found, and one of them moves back a little, the other drives forward, and they pass—Are these the people, as we believed for decades, in whom violence and cruelty are inbred and with whom there is no possibility of living in peace? What will we feel ten years from now when, let us hope, we walk through the streets of Damascus after making peace, and see the everyday faces of the people there, the Syrian eating with us in a restaurant, struggling mightily with the diet his wife has imposed on him, or when we read shy dedications inscribed in the books in a used book store, like the one I dug through in Cairo?

'We are not like the other Arabs,' the journalist Salwah Gamgum tells me. She is tall ('I am a large Pharaonic woman'), 'In particular, we are not like the Palestinians. We drink the waters of the Nile and learn peace and tolerance from them. The Nile flows softly in upper Egypt. It has no rapids and no currents.'

'You, the Israelis, are more like the Palestinians.' This is the opinion of Mahmad 'Ayn, twenty-six, with whom I drank potent, scorched tea by the pyramids. 'You are jumpy, excitable. One minute you feel like great heroes, and the next minute you are the most pathetic creatures in the world. Someone is always trying to cheat you. You are envious and materialist. We are not like that. We won't lift a finger for anything. That's why we look the way we do.' He laughed and waved his hand at the desert shimmering in the heat.

'We really are very different from you,' says Munir, a fluent speaker of Hebrew, who has visited Israel eleven times. 'There is no belligerence in us. There just isn't. We were ruined by the centuries of Ottoman rule. We have no energy. To this day—with the exception of a short period under Sadat—we live like we are still occupied by the Turks.'

'So what should you do in order to change?' I ask.

'Let the intellectuals plan our development, send—like the great Mohammed Ali did in his time—groups of students to Europe, to America. We need to become part of the modern world. Sadat was a man who knew how to give. Mubarak knows only how to receive. All the Arab leaders are like that. Nasser reinfected them all with that ancient disease, pan-Arabism, that gives us an excuse not to do anything except be led on by slogans. To passivity.'

'This moderation of the masses, that sometimes looks like apathy—'

'It *is* apathy. We don't have the internal strength you have. We only want life to go on without problems.'

'But it is very easy to exploit that apathy. We've seen how these same masses were carried away by Nasser's slogans.'

'I think,' he says cautiously, 'that today the situation is different. The multi-party system that Sadat introduced is continually getting stronger. Today Egyptian newspapers criticize Mubarak and survive. We have, even among the extremists who oppose Israel, a new feeling: we are different from the other Arabs in the region. That feeling will be hard to eradicate.'

He speaks loudly, enthusiastically. With his flashing eyes he looks like an Egyptian revolutionary from the beginning of the century, out to fight imperialism. We are in the large and magnificent mosque built by Mohammed Ali, and every voice is broken into six kinds of echo. Munir's Hebrew words bounce in every direction, but no one there is disconcerted.

Al-Fustat is where Cairo was born. Here, 1,350 years ago, Amar ibn el-'Ayin raised his tent, and here Egypt's first Muslim town was established. Today it is Cairo's rubbish dump. Trucks unload Cairo's trash here, and a brigade of children falls on each new pile. Every child picks out his speciality: some look for metal, others for glass, or wood and paper, or broken pottery. They take their finds home, to little clay and brick houses built on the mountains of refuse.

Curious three-year-olds with sores around their mouths surround me. They know the short-cuts and tunnels among the hills of trash and gladly lead me to their houses that are little sheds made of cardboard and crates. In the winter, they say, the rain comes in, but there isn't much rain here, only cold, and here the madame sleeps, and here the donkey, and on this mat all of us, we're ten, and this one, the little one, was once very, very lucky, a group of Americans came and saw him and decided to give him a scholarship, so that he can study, they even wrote down his name and sent it away, but probably some city official took the scholarship for himself.

Outside, in a few little pools, men stamp through brown water. They are separating the Nile clay from the oils in it, to prepare pottery. In the piercing sun they stand and churn the water. Tiny, skinny children scamper between them and pour out fresh water into the pools ('I am eleven, and old,' one water-carrier said to me). Inside a dusky lean-to, a huge man with lifeless eyes is stamping barefooted on a large block of clay. As he stamps he presses his knees with his hands and heavy sighs escape from his chest. His entire body and face are coated with clay from the block which coils around his calf muscles, so that muscles seem to swell out of the clay itself.

From there, quickly, back to the city, and the Khan el-Halili market where you can find everything: wooden clothes-pegs, sugar-cane juice, a special herb which allows you to clean your teeth in accordance with Koranic law, mummified hedgehogs and stuffed lizards to hang by your door for good luck. There are juicy miniature lemons, special tents in which mourners gather, a store for repairing shoe heels, and another one for soles, sparks fly out from under the knife-sharpener's wheel, cars emerge from both directions in the market alleys, and every second building is a mosque. In a puddle of blood and muck a slaughtered chicken convulses, its bulging eye seeing, upside down, the layers of fine wood, the *mashrabiat*, that cover the windows of the houses, through which modest women may look out, without being seen. Geese honk in reed cages, and a barefoot woman, treading through blood and raw sewage, waves another chicken, pinning its wings back and tying them together, to make it easier to weigh in the tin scale. A well-dressed man steps out of a restaurant, walks down the black street, every second or two sniffing on the tips of his fingers the rose water that was served him to wash his hands, and others have their meal around a *ful* wagon, wiping up beans and hummus with pitta bread, using a parked car as a table, and a yam-hawker slices a huge, hot, red, honey-sweet potato on a newspaper with a caricature of a thick-lipped Arafat stealing into a Zürich bank with bags of gold over his shoulders. You can't stand the Palestinians, I think at every meeting with Egyptians, so why do you fight so hard for them?

'We do not support the Palestinians out of love,' Tahsin Bashir tells me, 'but because of the issue itself. Because of the injustice itself, which could be righted and is not. Look—I visited Israel and I was prepared to go again, but the last time I was there, my heart was broken by the suffering, and it is hard for me to go back to that.'

'The behaviour of the Palestinian leadership is mistaken,' says Karima Kirolus, a reporter at *Al-Khabar,* 'but guilt lies only with the leadership. Had they a country, or hope for a country, they would not be swept away by every nationalist slogan.'

'We understand that it is hard for you to make peace with the Palestinians all at once.' This from Abd el-Satar Tawilah. 'But at least try to stop oppressing them so heavily. Try to treat them like the British treated you, and us. Let them demonstrate. Write. Protest. Strike. Try to understand their thinking and despair. Make little gestures. What will happen to you? After all, you are good at inventions and stratagems.'

'What do you care about negotiating with the Palestinians?' a friend of mine in Cairo heard from a well-known Egyptian statesman. 'Negotiations can go on for years. Sit down. Talk.

Argue. Break it up. Meet again. What can happen? What are you scared of? During the autonomy talks you proved that you know how to drag on negotiations, and no one punished you for it.'

'My advice to the Palestinian people,' wrote the editor of *Al Khabar*, Ibrahim Sa'adah, in a long, caustic article in which he railed against the prerogatives and 'free lunches' the Palestinians in Egypt still receive, 'is to ask all the governments that have hosted you, and brought your pain home to many, to hold conferences and congresses from which not one Palestinian will absent himself, and there announce your rejection of Arafat's position, and declare your lack of confidence in your whole gang of leaders, first and foremost that greatest acrobat of them all, Arafat. That is my faithful advice to you, and I am sure—may I be proven wrong—that you will refuse to take it.'

'But even when they refuse to take it, I will support them,' says Karima Kirolus, who speaks of principles in a fine and poetic Hebrew.

I stare suspiciously at these people, with an Israeli anger rising in me at the way Egyptians have exploited Palestinian suffering over the years to preserve the hatred against us. It is hard for me to believe that it's really just the good of the Palestinians that concerns them. It is hard for me to accept that they are not interested, more than anything else, in weakening Israel. But perhaps it is something ugly within me—within me only?—a sort of racism, the product of an Israeli Jewish education, that makes it difficult for me to believe that here, in the heart of filth and poverty, in the heart of the forbidding Arab world, humanitarian words about the need to find a solution to suffering and reduce injustice are being voiced sincerely.

'If the Palestinian problem were solved,' thinks Tarek el-Marshadi, an Egyptian student, 'your situation, in Israel, would be very different here. Everything is in your hands. You can decide today how the Arab world and Egypt will relate to you. And you are not doing anything. Nothing.'

Again and again the same voices: were the Palestinian problem solved, Israel would be tolerated as a partner in the

Middle East. Abstention from a solution shores up the impression among the Egyptians that the Israelis 'have not changed their ways,' that they are still interested in conquest and expansion. It is difficult to estimate to what extent this suspicion is rooted among them, and to what extent it is tied up with preconceptions about Jewish materialism, about the disloyalty and dishonesty that flows in Jewish blood.

The gulf between the psychologies of the two peoples is greatest, in my opinion, in the matter of the Six Day War. The Egyptians call that war 'the Israeli aggression'. I did not meet a single Egyptian who did not believe Israel was responsible for that war, and that had Israel not launched its pre-emptive attack, the war could have been prevented.

'Nasser never intended to go to war.' This is stated with utmost certainty by Abd el-Satar Tawila, author of the book *Israelis in Egyptian Eyes*. When he then told me 'Nasser never imagined how tense Israel was,' I recalled the two drivers in the alley in Cairo, face to face. They waited. Let the time go by. When one mediator failed—they waited for another one who was smarter and more patient than the first. Could it be that this was how the Egyptians saw the situation at the end of May 1967?

But how could the constricted Israel of June 1967, besieged, entirely mobilized, have been patient? And what about the October War, which the Egyptians started in 1973—the war that almost everyone here sees as a great victory?

After a few days in Egypt, I am prepared at least to try to see the reality of 1967 through their eyes, and to wonder whether the Six Day War might have been prevented. (A shattering sound spreads through my brain at those words.) The Six Day War—prevented? That most just of wars?

Could it be that more percipient leaders, more sober management of the waiting period that led up to the war, and, especially, our being more wisely and deeply attuned to the Egyptian character would have saved us all that blood? And all of what fell upon us after that war: the war of attrition, the occupation, the increasing isolation, the Yom Kippur War, the division of Israeli society?

'We'll make up with the Iraqis in the end,' A.H. said to me at the end of our conversation. 'Even though they betrayed us, we will be reconciled. That's the way it is in a family. You aren't part of our family. We'll accept you because you are here. We will do business with you, but you will not enter our hearts. You will remain outside.'

Whoever searches for love between us and the Arabs will be disappointed. He may despair. Whoever searches for a tolerable life and a conjunction of interests would do best to understand that things cannot be changed for the moment, and stop using them as eternal proof of hopelessness. He will do everything he can to strengthen the contacts, increase understanding, expose his protected world to a foreign way of thinking, so that his world will not again be surprised. So that it will not suddenly fall into the trap of war. And also, so that it will not miss a single new sapling of peace.

That is what I see from Cairo. These words are being written while I sit at the Israeli Academic Centre in Cairo. Little Israel on the Nile. Israelis and Egyptians work together here, under the intelligent management of Professor Yosef Ginat. A Coptic priest has just come in to order Bialik's and Ravnitzki's collection of rabbinic homilies and stories, *Sefer Ha-Agada*. We must not allow ourselves to forget such things, and we should never take them lightly.

'Perhaps you would indeed prefer that Israel not be here in the region at all? That the Middle East be entirely Arab?' I asked Munir at the modest farewell dinner, at the end of a taxing day of touring and talking.

He was taken by surprise. Something in him stirred, he blushed, and then he looked at me and said: 'Absolutely not. Without Israel we would be lost. Without Israel we would not have reason to liberate ourselves from our Arab disease. We Egyptians would remain like the Iraqis and the Iranians and the Syrians. Sometimes an accident or disaster changes your life. My father died when I was nine, and because of that disaster I was forced to enter the real world early, and I became something. Israel was a disaster for us, that is the truth. But it changed us. Israel showed us initiative, diligence and ambition. Everything we lack. Israel became our teacher and our competitor. Your country stopped being a misfortune and became a challenge.'

Translated from the Hebrew by Haim Watzman

Notes on Contributors

Mario Vargas Llosa grew up in Bolivia, was educated at a military academy in Peru—the experiences inform one of his early novels, *The Time of the Hero*—and has lived in Europe for more than twenty years. His many novels include *The War at the End of the World* and, most recently, *In Praise of the Stepmother.* A collection of his non-fiction writing will be published later this year. He lives in Lima and London. **Alvaro Vargas Llosa**, son of the novelist, was the press officer of *Libertad.* His account of the elections is selected from *El diablo en campaña* (*The Devil on Campaign*), a memoir of his father's campaign for president published in Spain and Latin America. **Mark Malloch Brown** is a member of the political consultancy Sawyer Miller. His account of advising Cory Aquino on her campaign for the presidency in the Philippines ('Aquino, Marcos and the White House') is published in *Granta* 18. **Sergio Larrain** was born in Chile in 1931 and studied in the United States. He returned to Chile in 1954 and was made a member of Magnum in 1959. **Sergio Ramirez**'s fiction includes short stories and the novel *To Bury our Fathers.* He has been invited to speak in Britain in October. **George Steiner**'s *Real Presences* has just been issued in paperback. 'Proofs', published here in an abridged form, will be included in a collection of his shorter fiction—all of which has appeared in *Granta*—that will be published by Faber & Faber next year. The first two parts of **Martin Amis**'s novel *Time's Arrow* were published in *Granta* 33 and 34. The book will be published later this year by Harmony Books in the United States and by Jonathan Cape in Britain. **T. Coraghessan Boyle**'s most recent novel is *East is East*. His last story published in *Granta* was 'The Miracle at Ballinspittle' (*Granta* 23). He lives in the San Fernando Valley in Los Angeles. 'Plastic' is from **Graham Swift**'s new novel, a work-in-progress, still untitled. He lives in south London. A new novel by **David Grossman** was published last spring in Israel. His most recent novel to be published in English is *The Smile of the Lamb*. He lives in Jerusalem with his family.